OVERVIEW

Overview

Everyone, at some point, has to negotiate. In fact, people negotiate almost daily to get what they want or need. The real trick to negotiation is to make both yourself and the other person happy. You may get what you want, but if you get it at the expense of your negotiation partner, your negotiation has failed. This course will show you ways to negotiate so that everyone leaves happy.

Many people view negotiation as something that diplomats and businessmen do in order to get what they want. While many of them no doubt approach negotiation with that mind-set, negotiation should be viewed as a collaborative, rather than competitive, process.

Negotiation is a process in which two or more parties with different needs and goals work together to find a solution that's acceptable to both.

In business, negotiation is a constant. In addition to negotiating deals or contracts, you'll need to negotiate with the people you work with on a daily basis.

Suppliers frequently ask for delays to deliver their products, buyers ask for extensions on payment, and employees ask for salary increases. Each of these requests requires negotiation skills to address properly.

If you can't negotiate through these issues, you won't survive in the workplace.

This course includes information you can use to become a better negotiator. You'll learn to recognize the actions that can help you negotiate successfully.

You'll learn about distinguishing between the two main types of negotiation: distributive and integrative.

And finally, you'll be introduced to the different styles of negotiation. Are you confrontational? Collaborative? Accommodating? This course will show you which style, or combination of styles, is the most appropriate in a given situation.

If you've ever tried to negotiate without being properly prepared, you may know firsthand what it's like to not get what you want. Consider Jose, who was honest and heartfelt when he told his boss, "My mortgage went up and my son needs braces. I need a raise!" Jose didn't plan for the negotiation, and only explained the situation from one point of view – his own. He didn't get the raise. But being prepared might have given him a better result.

In planning for negotiation, you have to figure out what you want and what the other side wants. You need to prepare for the give-and-take of negotiation, identifying areas of compromise and alternatives.

Negotiation Essentials

After all, an effective negotiation isn't a winner-take-all type of contest. Remember, many negotiations take place with people you need to work with after the negotiations are over.

Proper planning gives you the direction needed for effective problem solving at the negotiation table. In Jose's case, preparation could have helped him show how a raise would be a win-win solution.

Negotiation preparation allows you to be more confident, which gives you better control over the outcome. Preparation also gives you a greater understanding of the other party. This will help you craft a good solution.

In this course, you'll gain an understanding of the key considerations in preparing for negotiations.

You'll learn about determining overall goals and the needs, wants, and expectations of both sides of the negotiation. You'll also learn how to research the issues surrounding the negotiation and take into account the relationship you have with the other party.

You'll learn how to prepare for a negotiation by considering possible compromises you'll have to make and how to create negotiation value through trades. You need to research what outcomes would be good for both your interests and the other party's.

This course also covers how to identify the BATNA – which stands for best alternative to a negotiated agreement – in case a negotiation reaches an impasse.

You'll also learn how to determine your walk away point – otherwise known as the bottom line – and how to identify the area of common ground called the zone of possible agreement.

Negotiations, large and small, are part of daily life – whether you're at the bargaining table, negotiating an employment contract, haggling with a street vendor, or simply trying to get a child to eat vegetables. Although experts may disagree on the exact tactics to take to a negotiation session, all would no doubt agree that communicating effectively is key to a successful negotiation.

If you want a successful outcome in a negotiation, communication needs to be effective in both directions – your ideas, information, and message must be conveyed clearly, and you must understand the other party too.

In the not-too-distant past, negotiations frequently involved a no-holds-barred battle for advantage, with each side trying to get the most possible and to give up the least. But in modern business negotiations, the goal is more often a mutual win. This requires negotiators to make a connection with the person they're negotiating with; otherwise, it's unlikely an agreement will ever be reached.

Failure to effectively communicate can cost you the deal – the particular item you're negotiating for. But beyond that, in the modern business world, where relationships are of major importance, poor communication in a negotiation may cost you a relationship that's vital for your future.

In this course, you'll learn about communicating in a negotiation setting. The focus of the instruction is on three main areas: setting the tone, making effective proposals, and responding to the other party.

Setting the tone

You'll learn about the importance of setting the right tone for a negotiation and the ways to do so.

These include building rapport, keeping things focused on the positive aspects of the negotiation, and remaining consistent in tone throughout to inspire trust and confidence.

Making effective proposals

You'll learn about the crucial role of proposals in negotiation.

This includes the answers to questions such as "Who proposes first?", "How many issues should be dealt with at a time?", and "How should I structure my message for the best effect?"

You'll learn how to apply these tips and techniques using assertive language to make your needs clear and keep the discussion on a positive track.

Responding to the other party

You'll find out how to respond effectively in negotiations.

Techniques are explained, including how to avoid making an overly quick response, how to check your understanding, and ways of dealing with the emotional issues that may arise.

You'll also have an opportunity to practice using response techniques in a realistic scenario.

Using the information and techniques provided in this course, you'll enhance your understanding of the negotiation process. You'll also develop and improve your negotiation skills by learning about the important role of communication.

There's an old saying – "You can catch more flies with honey than you can with vinegar." This adage applies particularly well to negotiating. When you're negotiating with another party to find a mutually satisfying solution to a problem, a little honey can sweeten the proceedings and help you get what you want. The honey in the negotiations is persuasion.

Some people think that using persuasion in a negotiation is a little underhanded or shady. But persuasion can be used honestly and with the best of intentions. When you attempt to persuade someone, what you're trying to do is sway the other party to your way of thinking, your belief, or your position.

In order to do this, you first have to find out about the other party's way of thinking, beliefs, and positions. Then you can use what you know about the other person's wants and needs to engineer a mutually satisfying outcome to the negotiation.

In this course, you'll learn some persuasion techniques that can help you in any negotiation situation. In the first topic, you'll learn about putting yourself in the other party's position, building trust, and establishing a dialog. These three strategies are foundational to persuasive negotiating.

The second topic enables you to practice the three strategies from the first topic in a realistic roleplay.

And the third topic gives you some tips for dealing with difficult people, such as bullies, aggressive negotiators, and avoiders. It demonstrates how you can still be persuasive when faced with difficult behavior.

When you've completed the course, you'll have new and useful strategies and techniques in your negotiating toolkit. And you'll be better prepared in your next negotiation situation to persuade the other party to come around to your way of thinking.

Samuel is meeting with a new client today. He's never met Kendra before, but he's very confident of a good outcome. However, when Kendra walks into the room, she makes an unreasonable demand, pounds the table, and says, "Take it or leave it." Samuel is so surprised he makes an early concession. Then he becomes very competitive and determined to win at all costs. Both Samuel and Kendra soon lose their tempers. Before too long, Samuel walks out.

Negotiation is hard work, and it's filled with pitfalls, errors, and traps. For instance, failing to prepare adequately gives the other side the upper hand.

Overconfidence causes you to underestimate the other party and make false assumptions.

And if you're a competitive person, trying to beat the other party turns the negotiation into a battle you could easily lose.

Even the most seasoned negotiators make errors, but it's not inevitable you'll make them too. To become successful, you have to learn about the common pitfalls, errors, and traps and then learn about strategies for avoiding them.

In this course, you'll learn about common negotiating errors, including failing to prepare, succumbing to the urge to win, being overconfident, losing control of emotions, and limiting options. Then, you'll learn about strategies for avoiding and correcting these errors.

Next, you'll learn about negotiation traps, such as unreasonable demands, a take it or leave it attitude, inadequate authority, and last minute changes. Learning about these strategies for dealing with negotiation traps will help you avoid getting caught in them.

Finally, you'll find out how to diagnose barriers to agreement in a negotiation by looking at the design of the negotiation, the negotiation itself, and the pending deal.

By the time you've completed this course, you'll have learned about several excellent strategies for avoiding and recovering from negotiating pitfalls, errors, and traps.

CHAPTER 1 - WHAT IS NEGOTIATION

CHAPTER 1 - What Is Negotiation
  SECTION 1 - Negotiating Successfully
  SECTION 2 - Types of Negotiation
  SECTION 3 - Negotiation Styles

SECTION 1 - NEGOTIATING SUCCESSFULLY

SECTION 1 - Negotiating Successfully

Negotiation is a process that enables both parties to achieve, through discussion and compromise, a mutually acceptable objective. Participants benefit from negotiation by increasing their focus, satisfying their needs, and improving their relationships with others.

There are five actions you must take if you hope to have a successful negotiation: prepare well, set goals and limits, communicate clearly, control your emotions, and close the deal.

WHAT IS NEGOTIATION?

What is negotiation?

"In business, you don't get what you deserve, you get what you negotiate." This quote, by negotiation expert Chester L. Karrass, accurately sums up the importance of negotiation in achieving business goals. Negotiation involves a set of skills that are absolutely critical – not just for achieving your goals, but for your survival in the business world. In order to remain competitive in any business, you need to get the best possible deal. Getting that deal is only possible when you know how to negotiate.

What is negotiation? According to one dictionary definition, negotiation is "discussing or bargaining in order to reach agreement."

Most people have experience with some form of negotiation, although they may not realize it. It can be as minor as exchanging trading cards, as mundane as haggling over the price of paper products for the office, or as exciting and stressful as purchasing your first home.

Regardless of what form it takes, negotiation is something we all take part in at one time or another. In addition to knowing what negotiation is, it's important to know what it's not.

Negotiation is not selling, giving in, assessing blame, or arguing.

Nor is it a fight for dominance. Rather, it's an exchange that aims to find an agreeable solution for all interested parties. Approaching negotiation from a combative, win-at-all-costs perspective can be costly to both parties.

Negotiation can help prevent conflict or resolve existing conflict.

You can avert conflict if you agree to work with someone to find a mutually beneficial solution to an issue. In other words, negotiate with them rather than fight with them.

If done well, negotiation can strengthen the relationship between parties and lead to a deeper understanding and respect – which is especially important if a long-term relationship is desirable.

Question

Which of these best describe negotiation?

Options:

1. An exchange between two interested parties with the goal of reaching an agreement

2. A contest, where there are winners and losers

3. A quest, through dialog, to gain a competitive advantage over the person you're negotiating with

4. A survival skill that everyone in business needs to master

5. A way to prevent or deal with conflict

Answer

Option 1: This option is correct. Negotiation is a dialog that aims to reach an agreement suitable to both parties.

Option 2: This option is incorrect. Negotiation isn't combative, but rather a way for both sides to get what they want or need.

Option 3: This option is incorrect. You should view negotiation as an exchange of ideas rather than a competition.

Option 4: This option is correct. Negotiation enables you to get the best possible deal so that you can remain competitive.

Option 5: This option is correct. Everyone has to deal with conflict at some point, and negotiation is a way of managing conflict. It can also help you avert conflict by bringing together parties to seek a solution rather than to fight about a problem.

BENEFITS OF NEGOTIATING WELL

Benefits of negotiating well

Negotiation can be a frightening prospect for many people. It can be unpleasant if you go in unprepared, but there are a number of benefits if you approach negotiation correctly. By developing your negotiation skills, you'll sharpen your focus, satisfy your needs, and improve your relationships.

The first benefit of being able to negotiate is that it can sharpen your focus on what you want. As with most things, preparation is more than half the battle. Negotiating forces you to examine your position in a way you ordinarily might not.

If you look at your position from the other person's point of view, you may discover things that cause you to modify or refine your goals.

As a result, you may be able to communicate more clearly what you want.

The second benefit of negotiation is satisfying your needs. In a successful negotiation, your needs and the needs of the other party aren't mutually exclusive – in fact, they should be tied to each other. You may not always get exactly what you want, but by working in a collaborative fashion, you will at the very least walk away with your needs satisfied.

The third benefit of negotiation is improving your relationships with others. This benefit is often overlooked – in fact, many people don't consider it a part of negotiation. The old adage "strength in numbers" is particularly appropriate in negotiation.

By working together in a spirit of cooperation, both sides are able to achieve things that wouldn't be possible in isolation.

David works at a mid-sized IT firm that provides services to companies that lack the resources to employ a full-time IT person. Follow along as David negotiates with Li to sell her on his company's services.

David: From my research, I've noted that your company doesn't have a dedicated IT support helpdesk service. Can I ask why?

David is smiling.

Li: I know we should have something in place, but I've checked with various companies that provide that service, and I really don't see how we can afford it.

Li seems unconvinced.

David: I realize cost is an issue, but consider this: last year alone, eight out of ten companies failed to meet their project deadlines because their IT networks went down due to a software virus.

David looks concerned.

David: I believe we can tailor a solution for you that gives you what you need at a price you can afford.

David is smiling.

Li: Really? What kind of solution?
Li is pleasantly surprised.
David: Well, our basic package includes a number of services that will provide you with the security and 24-hour service you need, but at a substantially lower cost than our competitors. If, at a later date, you feel you need more service, we can upgrade you.
David is smiling.
Li: Wow, that sounds good. I've been worrying about this issue for a while now, and I like the idea of starting at a basic level and upgrading if necessary. Let's do it.
Li is pleased with the agreement.
David: Great. I took the liberty of writing up a service agreement based on my assessment. If this meets with your approval, I just need your signature and we can get started today.
David looks happy.
The exchange between Li and David illustrates some of the benefits of negotiation:

- David had done his homework and was prepared to address Li's concerns. This preparation enabled him to sharpen his focus and close the deal with Li.
- In the end, both sides were able to satisfy their needs. Li got the IT support her company needs at a price that fits her budget, and David was able to add Li's company as a client. As the company grows, so too will the need for IT support.
- By having a solution custom made for Li's company, David was able to improve their relationship through open and constructive

communication that demonstrated his concern for the company's particular needs.

Question

Which of these are benefits of being able to negotiate well?

Options:

1. Having your needs satisfied
2. Improving your relationship with others
3. Making you more determined and directed toward achieving your goal
4. Gaining an advantage over your negotiation partner
5. Giving in to the other party's demands

Answer

Option 1: This option is correct. While it may seem selfish to focus on satisfying your own side's needs, the needs of an organization are vital for its survival and growth. The key is to ensure that you don't achieve your goals at the expense of the other party.

Option 2: This option is correct. Negotiation focuses on finding agreeable solutions for all parties. When you negotiate well, both sides will make gains. You demonstrate that you're concerned about the other side's needs, which helps to strengthen the relationship.

Option 3: This option is correct. Negotiating can force you to examine your position, and provide you with the direction necessary to achieve your goals.

Option 4: This option is incorrect. Good negotiations are developed through building an agreeable solution for both parties.

Option 5: This option is incorrect. Giving in will not allow you to obtain a mutually satisfactory agreement.

FIVE ACTIONS FOR NEGOTIATING

Five actions for negotiating

In your response to what skills David showed in negotiating with Li, you may have included some or all of the five actions that can help you negotiate successfully. These actions are preparing well, setting goals and limits, communicating clearly, controlling your emotions, and closing the negotiation.

The most important of the five actions is preparation. Proper preparation is the foundation upon which all other actions are built, and should be done prior to entering the negotiation proceedings. In order to prepare well, you must consider the negotiation from three perspectives. You must consider yourself, the other person you are negotiating with, and the marketplace.

Yourself

Preparing yourself entails identifying your wants, needs, strengths, and weaknesses.

For example, are you an effective communicator? Do you sometimes have trouble clearly expressing yourself? Once you've identified those strengths and weaknesses, you can plan accordingly and work on clarifying your message in advance of negotiation.

The other person

Learn as much as possible about the person with whom you'll be negotiating. In addition to helping build a rapport with that person, you can determine what you're up against.

Is this person someone you can work with? Does this person have the authority to make a decision, or does a superior need to be involved? Knowing something about your negotiating partner also demonstrates that you've done your homework.

The marketplace

A solid understanding of the marketplace is essential. If it's your industry, you should know it as well or better than anyone. If it's an industry with which you're unfamiliar, then you need to research it and become as knowledgeable as possible.

Know the players, the terminology, and latest trends. Ask questions – it shows interest and a willingness to learn.

After considering the negotiation from the three perspectives, the next step is to set your goals and limits. This will help you avoid losing sight of your end goals.

You should document your goals, because it allows you to consider them in a concrete format, which makes them seem real. You can even post your goals in a place where you can refer to them daily, as a reminder of what you hope to achieve.

Setting limits enables you to identify where your cutoff point is. If you don't have a walk away position, you put yourself in danger of not only failing to achieve your goals, but also of losing what you currently have.

After all your preparation, you're ready to begin negotiating. During the negotiation, you'll need to be sure to communicate clearly and control your emotions so you can close the deal.

In order to communicate clearly during the negotiation phase, you should listen carefully. Many people think they're listening carefully when in fact they're simply waiting for their chance to speak.

Slow down, take a moment to absorb what you've learned, and think about the implications. Many people fail to do this. They continue to plow ahead and only later realize what they missed or misunderstood.

Take notes during the negotiation. Not only does this force you to slow down, but the act of writing down what you've just heard may help you absorb it more effectively. You'll also have the notes to refer back to at a later date.

Speaking clearly is the key to effective communication. As with listening, many people think they are effective communicators when in fact they aren't. This can be difficult to accept, and requires a great deal of self-evaluation to fix. You should ask people close to you for feedback on your communication skills. Are there things that you do that distract your listeners from what you're saying? Do you present a consistent message in the way you communicate?

Be careful to stay focused on your message. Refer back to the goals and limits you set for yourself and use them as a guide during negotiation so you won't stray. Some people have a tendency to wander off subject during discussions. As a result, they confuse not only themselves, but the people they're negotiating with. If you find the other person drifting off topic, ask questions to clarify what they mean and get back on track.

Question

Now that you've learned about the first three negotiation skills, demonstrate your understanding of these skills. Match each action with its corresponding characteristic.

Options:

A. Prepare well
B. Set goals and limits
C. Communicate clearly

Targets:

1. Consider the negotiation from the perspective of yourself, the person you are negotiating with, and the marketplace
2. Identify where your cutoff point is
3. Slow down, take notes, and think about the implications of what's being said

Answer

In order to prepare well, you must consider the negotiation from these three perspectives.

If you don't set goals and limits, including your cutoff point, you put yourself in danger of failing to achieve your goals.

Many people think they're listening carefully when in fact they're simply waiting for their chance to speak. Listening will help you communicate clearly.

Another action critical to success in negotiation is controlling your emotions. Controlling your emotions prevents you from doing or saying things that might place the negotiation in jeopardy.

Consider the analogy of brakes on a car. Without brakes, you'd certainly crash your car. Some situations call for a gentle press of the brakes, while others require very sudden and very hard braking.

Controlling your emotions during a negotiation is very much like those brakes. Sometimes touching the brakes lightly – for example, by saying nothing at the right moment – can prevent you from saying something that weakens your argument. At other times, you may have to hit the brakes much harder.

In the same way that reading a street sign might prevent an accident, controlling your emotions is easier when you know what might upset you or cause you to stumble. If you've taken the time to prepare, you'll know if there are specific sticking points or issues that could disrupt the negotiation. Being prepared for these situations means you'll know the right moment to apply the brakes and avoid problems during the negotiation.

The final action required for a successful negotiation is the ability to close the deal.

Closing the deal can be the point where negotiations fall apart. If not handled correctly, all your time and effort can be wasted. There are a few key points to remember in order to successfully close a negotiation.

As with controlling your emotions, success in closing the negotiation also involves putting on the brakes at the right moment. In this case, however, you may need to apply the brakes and steer your car around obstacles at the same time to reach your destination.

If you've spent any time negotiating, you've run across people who use a variety of tactics to swing things in their favor. Regrouping can give you a chance to get out of a corner you're being forced into and develop strategies for dealing with these kinds of tactics. It also allows you time to cool off and not make any hasty decisions. This can be key when it comes to making a deal that benefits both you and the other party.

Listening and clearly stating your position are also important for a successful close to a deal. Sometimes it seems as though the other person is being difficult when in fact it's a case of not being heard. In other situations, the disconnect may be due to the fact that you haven't clearly stated your wants and needs.

Closing the deal is where everything comes together in the negotiation. Ideally, you want to close the deal as quickly and as smoothly as possible. If you've successfully navigated through the negotiation process using the other four actions, you're now in a position to reach an agreement.

Successful negotiation requires careful implementation of all five actions. By preparing well and setting goals and limits, the pieces are in place to begin negotiation. Communicating clearly and controlling your emotions are essential to closing the deal.

They may not always bring about an agreement, but these five actions are the most effective and direct path to reaching an agreement that meets the needs of both sides.

Question

Which actions are essential to success in negotiation?

Options:

1. Becoming familiar with the industry and the person with whom you'll be negotiating

2. Identifying how far you're willing to go in terms of price, and making sure it's the product you want

3. Clearly expressing your wants and needs, and paying attention to the wants and needs of the other side

4. Hard selling your idea to your negotiation partner

5. Controlling the negotiation to ensure your needs are met 6. Putting the brakes on your emotions

Answer

Option 1: This option is correct. To succeed in negotiation, you need to prepare. Part of that preparation requires that you become familiar with the industry in question, as well as the needs and interests of the person you're negotiating with.

Option 2: This option is correct. Setting goals and limits on such things as price, product, and timelines is essential to success in a negotiation.

Option 3: This option is correct. Negotiation is an exchange of ideas, products, and services. This is only possible when both sides are communicating clearly.

Option 4: This option is incorrect. Hard selling isn't the right approach for all negotiations. It's true that selling skills may be used during negotiation, but selling is not one of the five actions essential to success in negotiation.

Option 5: This option is incorrect. While it's important to satisfy your needs, controlling a negotiation is generally not possible – nor desirable.

Option 6: This option is correct. One of the most common techniques for controlling your emotions is "putting the brakes on" when you feel you're losing control.

SECTION 2 - TYPES OF NEGOTIATION

SECTION 2 - Types of Negotiation

Conflict in business is unavoidable. In fact, business is built on the premise of competition between the various players – buyers are looking for the best price, and sellers are looking to make a profit. In order to survive in this environment, negotiation is essential.

There are two main types of negotiation: distributive and integrative. In distributive negotiation, a gain by one side represents a loss to the other. The practitioners of this type of negotiation act accordingly. Integrative negotiation, on the other hand, involves collaboration and uses creative ways for both sides to benefit.

WHY NEGOTIATION IS NECESSARY

Why negotiation is necessary

Conflict is inevitable. Regardless of the environment, there are always differences of opinion. The irony is that as a workplace becomes more collaborative, it also becomes an environment where conflict can flourish. This may seem like a negative, but in fact it's just the opposite – if managed correctly.

Conflict is perfectly natural. Children display this behavior when they fight over a toy. Fortunately, in most cases, an adult is there to act as a mediator. As adults, we have to rely on our ability to negotiate to get what we want or need.

There are many ways to win at negotiation, but they needn't be at the expense of others. In addition to gaining what you want – more money or a better price, for example – there are benefits to building a relationship through negotiation.

Negotiation can reveal previously hidden opportunities for both sides:

- in cases of conflicts inside an organization, negotiation can strengthen the structural links that exist between people and departments, and
- in cases of negotiation between organizations, each side may discover that the other has useful strengths or resources and that both can benefit from an exchange or partnership.

Imagine for a moment that you work with someone who is responsible for collecting information and recording it in reports. You need these reports in order to complete your job, yet this person is consistently omitting crucial information or entering it incorrectly, making your job more difficult.

Given the seriousness of the problem, you must confront this person. In situations like this, negotiation skills are critical.

If you take an accusatory approach instead of approaching the situation as a negotiation, you risk creating animosity with your coworker and making the situation worse.

While negotiation is an ideal strategy for handling conflict, there are some nonproductive ways of dealing with conflict that should be avoided. These include denial, escalation to a higher authority, capitulation, and passive-aggressive behavior.

Denial

This attitude prevents natural, constructive conflict from happening and limits any growth or opportunity that may have resulted from that conflict.

This may work, if the person to whom the issue has been escalated handles it correctly. Unfortunately, in many cases, it simply results in the issue being swept under the rug.

Escalation to a higher authority

Some people choose to avoid conflict or act as though it isn't there. They believe that because everyone is on the same team, conflict shouldn't exist.

In order to avoid conflict, many people simply escalate the matter to a higher authority. Their attitude is, "Let someone else deal with it."

Capitulation

Many people give in when faced with conflict. This occurs when individuals trade their wants and needs for peace in the workplace.

By avoiding conflict, they're not helping themselves in a troublesome situation, and they're preventing positive change from occurring.

Passive-aggressive behavior

Passive-aggressive behavior is possibly the most destructive response to conflict. Instead of confronting or avoiding conflict, people pretend they're OK with the status quo or proposed change, but then continue behaving in the way that caused the conflict in the first place.

Not only does this behavior postpone conflict resolution, it creates a toxic environment that makes future negotiation more difficult.

Question

Which are examples of productive outcomes of dealing with conflict through negotiation?

Options:

1. Getting what you want
2. Assigning responsibility for problems that exist

3. Improving relationships
4. Staking out boundaries

Answer

Option 1: This option is correct. Conflict, if handled in a professional manner through negotiation, can help you achieve your goals.

Option 2: This option is incorrect. While it may be satisfying on occasion to be proven right, assigning blame for problems or mistakes only leads to animosity, which can make negotiation more difficult.

Option 3: This option is correct. By handling conflict in a professional manner – through negotiation – relationships can be strengthened to the benefit of all involved.

Option 4: This option is incorrect. Many people use conflict in the workplace to protect their "territory" or to intimidate others. This approach creates a toxic work environment and negatively impacts productivity.

TYPES OF NEGOTIATION

Types of negotiation

Some people approach negotiation as a confrontation – the idea that "what's mine is mine and what's yours is negotiable."

Others know the value of working with the other side to achieve a mutually beneficial solution. Some people approach negotiation as a confrontation – the idea that "what's mine is mine and what's yours is negotiable."

Others know the value of working with the other side to achieve a mutually beneficial solution.

Distributive

Distributive negotiation is a way of dividing up a single, fixed quantity where a gain to one side results in a loss to the other. While both sides may benefit from the deal, one side will definitely benefit more than the other.

Integrative

Integrative negotiation involves a more collaborative approach, where both sides work together in the hopes of achieving the greatest possible benefit for both sides.

Even in a negotiation where there's direct competition between the two sides, there are often opportunities for collaboration. It's rare to find a negotiation that's purely distributive or purely integrative. Most fall somewhere in between, but it's important to understand each type on its own.

Distributive negotiation is often referred to as "zero-sum" negotiation. Its goal is the acquisition of value. At the end of the negotiation, the person who can claim the most value is the winner.

Think of it in terms of a poker game. The first offer is critical because it sets the bargaining range, so you need to start at the right place. Once the game begins, both sides keep their cards close to their vest, taking care not to reveal too much information to the other side. The goal is to win as much as possible.

Situations where distributive negotiation might be used

Distributive negotiation is often used in situations where there's a single, fixed issue to be negotiated, and where the greatest concern is getting the best possible value. You may have thought of situations such as buying an expensive item such as a car or a house, or perhaps bartering a price for an antique.

In the pages that follow, as you learn more about the characteristics of distributive negotiation, you'll probably get more insight into situations where it might be useful.

A key difference between the two types of negotiation is how information is handled in distributive negotiation. In distributive negotiation, the goal is to withhold as much information as possible, putting the other side at a disadvantage.

For example, if a customer was aware that you had a surplus of a particular product taking up room in your warehouse, that customer could use the information to push you for a lower per-unit price. It's also important to try to find out as much information as you can about the other side, to create a greater advantage for yourself.

For example, say your international company is interested in buying a small building for a new branch office. You've recently discovered that a building you're interested in is owned by a company that is in a hurry to sell because they've already purchased another building. You use this information to your advantage by offering less than the asking price, but setting the closing date sooner rather than later.

Your company just might be on its way to becoming the new owner of this building.

In distributive negotiation, future relationships are not a priority. In a purely distributive negotiation, you'll likely never meet with your negotiating opponent again. Take, for example, buying a new car. When you buy a car, your primary concern isn't usually your long-term relationship with the salesperson or the dealership. It's how much you are going to have to pay for the car you want. Your relationship with this person is typically the farthest thing from your mind.

Question

What are characteristics of distributive negotiation?

Options:

1. Getting the most value is all that matters
2. Future relationships are a priority
3. Safeguarding information is essential
4. The first offer is critical

5. Sharing of information is encouraged

Answer

Option 1: This option is correct. In distributive negotiation, the goal is to get as much as possible.

Option 2: This is an incorrect option. Relationships aren't important in distributive negotiation. The goal is to get as much as you can and move on.

Option 3: This is a correct option. Information is critical in distributive negotiation. The goal is to learn as much as you can about the other side, and keep your own cards close to your vest.

Option 4: This option is correct. The first offer is critical because it sets the bargaining range.

Option 5: This option is incorrect. Sharing of information is not encouraged in distributive negotiation. For example, you may be in a hurry to sell, and that information could be used by the other side to pressure you to accept a lower price.

In purely integrative negotiation, both sides cooperate to achieve the greatest benefit. This type of negotiation requires that you be good at both creating value and claiming it.

Your goal is to create as many options with as much value as possible for both sides.

And then you need to claim the best value for yourself among the options you've helped create. This can result in both sides getting exactly what they want, but in most cases it requires that each side compromise slightly to get what it values the most.

So instead of trying to get the biggest piece of the pie, or focusing on a single issue, you consider other options –

other types of value. The more options you have, the more likely you'll be able to claim value in the negotiation.

Parties in integrative negotiations seek creative options rather than focusing on which concessions to make.

Unlike in distributive negotiation, to be successful at integrative negotiation, you need to share information. There are several ways negotiators can do this:
- discuss key issues related to their situation, including why they want to make a deal and what their real interests are, as well as their business constraints,
- be up-front about their preferences among options and issues, and
- reveal any additional resources or capabilities that match the other side's interests.

Question

What are the characteristics of integrative negotiation?

Options:

1. Both parties communicate their real interests
2. A single issue is usually the focus of negotiations
3. The goal is to create maximum value for both sides
4. Sharing of information is encouraged
5. The first offer is critical
6. You need to be good at creating value and claiming it

Answer

Option 1: This option is correct. Integrative negotiation is more successful when parties share information, such as their real interests or business constraints.

Option 2: This option is incorrect. Integrative negotiations focus on various issues in order to find creative options that meet the interests of both parties.

Option 3: This option is correct. Integrative negotiation seeks to "enlarge the pie," so that each side can then claim value.

Option 4: This option is correct. Information plays an important role in both types of negotiation, but integrative negotiation requires that the parties share rather than safeguard information.

Option 5: This option is incorrect. The first offer is not critical in integrative negotiation, as the negotiation is based less on bargaining and more on collaboration.

Option 6: This option is correct. In integrative negotiation, you need to be able to create as many types of value as you can for both parties, and then you need to claim the best value among the options for yourself.

SELECTING THE RIGHT NEGOTIATION TYPE

Selecting the right negotiation type

The question at this point is "What is the most appropriate negotiation type – distributive or integrative?" There are pros and cons for each type. The most common analogy for these two types of negotiations is the pie. In the case of distributive negotiation, the pie represents the whole of what's available, and each side fights to get as much of it as possible. Integrative negotiation looks to enlarge the pie so that both sides get what they need.

Integrative negotiation may seem to be the weaker of the two types. After all, distributive negotiation is about going after what you want while protecting what you have, whereas integrative negotiation requires negotiators to consider the interests of the other side. However, integrative negotiation isn't negotiating from a position of weakness, but is rather a way to create and claim value. It says "Let's work together on this. We'll both benefit, but here's what I want out of the deal."

It may seem as though distributive negotiation has no place outside a fixed value negotiation, but it often plays a role in integrative negotiations. Distributive negotiation comes into play in the "claiming value" portion of integrative negotiation.

If the creating value portion of the integrative negotiation has created a bigger pie, then claiming value through distributive negotiation can be profitable for both sides.

And if the first part of the integrative negotiation is unsuccessful, due to lack of creativity or lack of cooperation, then the pie may not be large enough for both sides to divide amicably. In this case, the negotiation will resemble a purely distributive negotiation.

Most negotiations should be handled using an integrative approach, as it has more potential for creating lasting agreements and relationships. There will, however, always be negotiations in which a distributive approach will yield results, and it can also play a part in an integrative negotiation, when appropriate.

Question

Match the types of negotiation with their corresponding characteristics. Each negotiation type may match to more than one characteristic.

Options:

A. Distributive negotiation
B. Integrative negotiation

Targets:

1. A single issue will be the focus of the negotiation
2. Information sharing is encouraged
3. Collaboration is the most important factor
4. Safeguarding information is critical

5. A gain by one side represents a loss to the other
Answer

In distributive negotiation, both sides are fighting over a fixed quantity. Creativity and long-term relationships are not as important as the issue being negotiated.

Sharing information is a key characteristic of integrative negotiation. By sharing information, opportunities for mutual benefit can be revealed. If this information is guarded, these opportunities can be missed.

Integrative negotiation is based on the premise of collaboration. By working together, the two sides can develop a solution based on their needs and find ways of addressing those needs.

Practitioners of distributive negotiation prefer to keep their cards close to their vest. This can be useful in a confrontational type of negotiation, but it can limit both short-term and long-term opportunities for both sides.

Purely distributive negotiation generally results in clear winners and losers, as both sides are fighting over a specific prize.

SECTION 3 - NEGOTIATION STYLES

SECTION 3 - Negotiation Styles
Negotiation style refers to the general approach or behavioral style you use in negotiating. The negotiating style you use in a given situation can make the difference between success and failure. Negotiation styles can be broken into five distinct categories, or characteristics: avoiding, accommodating, collaborating, compromising, and competing.

Matching the appropriate negotiation style to a given situation is essential to a successful negotiation. The primary consideration in selecting the correct negotiation style is determining where a particular issue falls in terms of its importance. This is accomplished by looking at the relative importance of the relationship between the two parties versus the importance of the outcome of the negotiation.

IDENTIFYING YOUR NEGOTIATION STYLE

Identifying your negotiation style

How would you describe your personality type? Some people are naturally friendly, while others are more reserved. Your personality type dictates how you interact with the world around you, and it impacts everything from the friendships you form to the type of job you have – and how successful you are at that job.

Negotiation style is very much the same, in that it refers to the general approach or behavioral style you use in negotiating.

The negotiating style you use in a given situation can make the difference between success and failure.

To illustrate the importance of negotiation style, imagine using the same style in two very different situations. Suppose you're buying a single company car for a small company. Your only goal is to get the best price – you refrain from sharing information and don't worry about making the other side happy.

Now imagine you're negotiating with a union on behalf of the government. Taking a hard line with the union could push the union into a strike position – a position from which no one benefits.

If negotiation style wasn't an issue, then the direct, confrontational approach should have worked in both situations. The lesson learned is that you need to adjust your negotiation style to suit the situation.

If you're confrontational by nature, then you need to learn to adapt to situations where that approach can alienate the other side. If you're reserved by nature, you need to become more assertive in the face of aggressive people. The key in both situations is to know which style a given negotiation calls for, and to apply that style to maximum effect.

Question

Before you learn about the various negotiation styles, it's important to identify your own inherent negotiation style. By identifying, and acknowledging, your own negotiation style, you can learn how to modify your style and perhaps avoid slipping back into it when it may not be appropriate.

How would you describe your negotiating style?

Options:

1. I prefer a direct, no-nonsense approach

2. I generally try to find common ground in negotiations

3. I avoid confrontation by giving in soon after the negotiation starts

Answer

Option 1: This approach can be very effective in negotiations where relationships don't matter, but if you always take an aggressive approach, you risk alienating the other side in other negotiation situations.

Option 2: Taking a collaborative approach is often the correct negotiation style, but there are certain situations in which you'll need to be less collaborative and more competitive.

Option 3: While concessions are sometimes necessary for a successful negotiation, simply giving in can set a damaging precedent if you're planning on a long-term relationship.

Negotiation styles can be broken into five distinct categories, or characteristics: avoiding, accommodating, collaborating, compromising, and competing. Before you enter a negotiation, you need to decide which style is most appropriate. This can depend on the relationship you have with the other party, and on the importance you or the other party place on the outcome. While it's true that collaborating is often the most appropriate style, sometimes adopting another approach can help you achieve the best result.

In certain negotiations, the outcome is of primary importance. This situation is most clearly illustrated in a new car purchase, where the relationship with the salesman is often of little or no importance and price is the motivating factor.

In some negotiations, the relationship takes precedence. At certain points in a negotiation, you may negotiate things that aren't important to you, but are very important to the other side. As part of securing what you want, you need to ensure that the other side is able to get what they need. Determining the most appropriate negotiation style in a given scenario, therefore, requires identifying where that scenario fits in terms of the emphasis it places on the relationship and the outcome.

AVOIDING

Avoiding
Have you ever been engaged in a negotiation where you had little or no relationship with the other side, and you really weren't that committed to the outcome?
Question
For example, suppose you're a project manager with a number of employees and resources under your control. A new project manager needs two of your employees for his first project, and promises you something in return. You're not interested in creating a relationship with him or in what he has to offer.

By referring to the chart, which of the negotiation styles seems most appropriate in this situation?

The negotiation style matrix ranks the styles on an x and y axis, with the vertical axis representing the importance of the relationship and the horizontal axis representing the importance of the outcome. Avoiding occupies the corner block, indicating a low importance of both the relationship and the outcome. For Accommodating, the importance of the outcome is low but there's an increased emphasis on the relationship. Compromising and competing each have an equally low importance of relationship to avoiding, but have an increasing importance of outcome. Collaborating has a high importance of relationship and a high importance of outcome.

Options:
1. Avoiding
2. Accommodating
3. Collaborating
4. Compromising

Answer

If the relationship or outcome are important to you, you'll be motivated to negotiate. Here, neither is important to you.

Avoiding is a style of negotiation where both the relationship and the outcome are unimportant to you. As a result, you either withdraw or avoid negotiating.

In the preceding example, avoiding the other project manager appears to be easier than explicitly stating that you aren't interested. You may not want to create unnecessary friction, but you don't want to trade with this project manager because you don't feel you have anything of real value to gain from it.

Avoiding may take a number of forms, such as sidestepping an issue, postponing a meeting, or withdrawing from contact with the other person. In all cases, a lack of interest for both the relationship and the outcome is the cause.

Avoiding as a preferred negotiation style is generally rare. It typically happens by default – one or both sides aren't interested in negotiating and try to find ways to avoid it.

ACCOMMODATING

Accommodating

An accommodating style is typically used in situations where you value the relationship over the outcome of the negotiation. The goal is to make the other side happy. The downside to this approach is that in your attempt to please the other side, you risk losing what you really want or need.

Sonya is negotiating with Michael, a salesman for a company that manufactures batteries for the ride-on lawn tractors that Sonya's company builds. The two companies have worked together for years and have a very solid relationship. One aspect of the negotiation is the price per unit, which Sonya would like to have reduced by approximately 10%.

Sonya

"We really need to get you to move on price a little – how about 10%?"

Michael

"I'd really like to help you, but we have to stand firm on price in order for us to turn a profit. We've been doing business a long time, and we really want to make you happy, but we just can't go any lower."

Sonya meets with her boss, Cynthia, following the negotiation with Michael to report on how things went. When the subject of price per unit comes up, Cynthia is concerned with the firm stand Michael has taken. Follow along as Sonya and Cynthia discuss their options in light of Michael's position.

Sonya: I pushed very hard on this point. I realize how important it is for us to cut costs right now, but he was adamant.

Cynthia: What do you think? Should we consider looking for another supplier?

Sonya: I don't think so. I believe Michael is telling the truth when he says they can't make a profit if they charge less. The other thing to consider is our relationship with his company.

Sonya: Do you remember the time we had a problem with the battery size in that prototype, and how quickly they helped us find a workable solution? Our designers love working with them. I don't think we'll find another company like that for less money.

Cynthia: Agreed. We'll just have to live with the current price. Thanks Sonya.

Cynthia is smiling.

Not all accommodating negotiations are as positive as illustrated in this example. Relationships are important, and being accommodating on occasion is necessary, but it's also important that you get what you need. If you're being accommodating on certain issues, the other side should do the same on other issues.

COLLABORATING

Collaborating
Question
Collaborating is an even mix in terms of the importance of relationship versus outcome. In other words, both sides care strongly about the issue and care about and respect each other.

Which type of negotiation is the collaborating negotiation style most like?
Options:
1. Distributive
2. Integrative

Answer
Collaboration is the style associated with integrative negotiation, in which participants value both the relationship and the outcome.

Option 1: Distributive negotiation is characterized by a high expectation for outcome, and a low expectation for relationship. Collaboration is the opposite of that.

Option 2: Integrative negotiation is characterized by a desire to balance the relationship with the outcome.

Notice that the collaborative style spans the mid to high range on both factors.

The most effective of the five negotiation styles, collaborating is where relationship meets outcome.

In this negotiation style, both sides try to maximize their outcomes while preserving or enhancing the relationship. This is generally the best approach for most negotiations, but can only occur when both sides can find a way to meet their needs.

Collaboration is based on trust and mutual concern for the other side. If one side doesn't have this same concern, then trust will soon break down and the dynamic of the negotiation will change.

Consider this example of collaboration. You work at a toy manufacturer, and you have an existing relationship with a distributor who buys your train sets.

The managers of the distributing company love your product, and are always open and eager to work with you on all issues. When you raise your concerns, they listen carefully, ask thoughtful questions, and are quick to suggest ways of bridging any gaps.

Their approach leaves you feeling that they can be trusted and will be more than willing to work with you. As a result, you feel confident sharing information and working with them to get the best deal for all concerned.

Question

Now that you've learned about the first three negotiation styles, demonstrate your understanding of when to use each style.

Match each style with its corresponding description.

Options:
A. Accommodating

B. Avoiding
C. Collaborating

Targets:

1. You value the relationship over the outcome
2. Both the relationship and the outcome are unimportant to you
3. You value the relationship and the outcome equally

Answer

Accommodating places a premium on relationships. The risk is that by placing so little emphasis on the outcome, you won't get what you want or need.

When you don't care about the relationship or the outcome, you may avoid the negotiation altogether. If it's not worth the effort, then you may retreat from the situation.

Collaborating happens when one or both sides attempt to fully satisfy the needs of both parties.

COMPROMISING

Compromising
One of the most commonly used negotiation styles, compromising, is appropriate when neither side can achieve full collaboration, but each still hopes to achieve a portion of their desired outcome.

Compromising places slightly more value on the outcome than the relationship. The downside to compromising is that it sometimes forces both sides into extreme positions. Knowing that the other side will be looking for concessions, each side will raise their stakes.

Compromise may also be used in situations where both parties are under pressure to reach a quick resolution or take some action to preserve the relationship. In some cases, compromise may be used when both parties can't, or won't, make the effort to work toward a fully collaborative agreement.

Compare your experience using compromise in a negotiation situation with this example. Jim is the owner of an auto body shop, and he's been buying paints from the same supplier for the past 10 years. He recently discovered that another company can provide him with the same products, but for less money.

He meets with representatives of his regular supplier to see if they can lower their prices. If they can't, he'll have to go with the competitor. They agree to lower their prices, but they don't quite match the competitor's prices.

Jim agrees to the new prices, as he'd prefer to maintain the relationship if possible. But then they come back with a request of their own: instead of billing every 3 months, they want to start billing on a monthly basis. This will increase their monthly cash flow.

In this case, both sides may have to give up something to get something. Instead of being rigid and insisting on getting what they want, each side can come away with something.

Although the relationship isn't a top priority in a compromising negotiation, it's a factor, and is important enough to consider when deciding whether to accept certain concessions.

In some cases, the outcome could have more importance than the relationship in a compromising approach. If that's the case, you may find that your negotiation falls somewhere in the middle of the scale, between an integrative and distributive type of negotiation.

Compromising is similar to collaborating, except that, when compromising, negotiators don't change their viewpoints or create new ones. Compromising means both sides gain and lose. Collaborating occurs when one or both parties try to fully satisfy the needs of both parties.

COMPETING

Competing

The last negotiation style is competing, also known as distributive negotiation. This style places all the emphasis on the outcome. In this style of negotiation, relationships don't matter. Some people believe this to be the best style for negotiating, where both sides go "toe to toe" in an effort to get what they can from each other. In some cases, this may be necessary, but there are very few instances where the relationship doesn't matter.

Consider this example of a competitive negotiation. You work for a company that renovates and resells older properties. You've been instructed by your boss to purchase another property, but you're finding it difficult to find something in your price range.

Your boss tells you about a place where the owner is in a hurry to sell because she's purchased another house and the closing date is approaching.

When you meet with the real estate agent, you use the information you have to negotiate a lower price, but you stipulate that you want to close immediately. You don't mention that you know the homeowner's predicament.

This example illustrates a few key points associated with the competing style of negotiation. As you aren't likely to ever meet the homeowner, the relationship isn't a factor in this negotiation. Also, having, but not sharing, important information gives you the edge in the negotiation. In any negotiation, information is power, but in this competitive style of negotiation, information is used as a tool to gain an advantage over the other side.

Question Set

Now that you've learned about all five styles of negotiating, you'll have a chance to see if you can recognize them in use.

The negotiation style matrix ranks the styles on an x and y axis, with the vertical axis representing the importance of the relationship and the horizontal axis representing the importance of the outcome. Avoiding occupies the corner block, indicating a low importance of both the relationship and the outcome. For Accommodating, the importance of the outcome is low but there's an increased emphasis on the relationship. Compromising and competing each have an equally low importance of relationship to avoiding, but have an increasing importance of outcome. Collaborating has a high importance of relationship and a high importance of outcome.

Question 1 of 2

Brad and Melissa have been negotiating the purchase of Brad's company. The negotiation has been going back and forth for weeks, and most of the details have been worked out at this point. But there's still one last issue:

Melissa wants to keep the company name, but Brad is reluctant. In the end, he agrees to allow Melissa to retain the company name. In return, Melissa pays a price a little closer to Brad's original asking price.

Which negotiation style did Brad and Melissa adopt in this situation?

Options:

1. Avoiding
2. Accommodating
3. Collaborating
4. Compromising
5. Competing

Answer

Option 1: This option is incorrect. Avoidance indicates a low importance of both relationship and outcome, but that's clearly not the case in this scenario.

Option 2: This option is incorrect. Both sides were looking to get something from the other, which indicates that the focus was leaning more towards outcome.

Option 3: This option is incorrect. In this scenario, the focus was a less on the relationship and a little more on the outcome.

Option 4: This is the correct option. Both sides were willing to give a little to get what they really wanted.

Option 5: This option is incorrect. Both sides were willing to concede certain things, which would eliminate competing as the negotiating style.

Question 2 of 2

Bob is negotiating with an auto parts company that manufactures brake pads. The parts company is looking to increase the price of its pads by $1.50. Bob wants to negotiate a slightly lower price, but the parts company isn't willing to budge because of an increase in the price of raw materials. A lower price would force the company to sell at a loss, so getting the higher price is of the utmost importance. When Bob offers a buying price 75 cents lower per part, the company refuses. They state that they aren't offering a price lower than what they quoted, and that Bob can take it or leave it. Bob is interested in maintaining the relationship with the company, so he gives them the price they want.

Which negotiation style did the parts company adopt in this situation?

Options:
1. Avoiding
2. Accommodating
3. Collaborating
4. Compromising
5. Competing

Answer

Option 1: This option is incorrect. Avoidance indicates a low importance of both relationship and outcome, but the parts company is very interested in the outcome of this negotiation.

Option 2: This option is incorrect. Bob uses an accommodating approach here, but the parts company does not.

Option 3: This option is incorrect. Although the parts company may value the relationship, it values the outcome – the price of the pads – more in this case and isn't willing to budge.

Option 4: This option is incorrect. The parts company isn't willing to lose anything on this negotiation, so they aren't adopting a compromising approach, which requires a loss and gain for each party.

Option 5: This is the correct option. The parts company is interested in the outcome and so adopts a competing approach.

CHAPTER 2 - PLANNING FOR NEGOTIATION

CHAPTER 2 - Planning for Negotiation
 SECTION 1 - Researching for a Negotiation
 SECTION 2 - Prepare for Compromises in a Negotiation
 SECTION 3 - Know Your BATNA and "Walk Away" Point in a Negotiation

SECTION 1 - RESEARCHING FOR A NEGOTIATION

SECTION 1 - Researching for a Negotiation

When you're prepared for a negotiation, you'll be more confident, which leads to better control over the outcome. Preparation also leads to a better understanding of the other party, which makes negotiations easier. And when your requirements – and those of the other party – are well defined, you'll have an easier time crafting a solution that needs few modifications later on.

Key considerations in preparing for negotiations are determining what your overall goal is and what your needs, wants, and expectations are. You'll also need to gather information about the needs, wants, and expectations of the other party, the issues surrounding the negotiation situation, and the type of relationship you have with the other party.

PREPARING FOR NEGOTIATIONS

Preparing for negotiations

Have you ever been part of a negotiation where someone wasn't prepared? Was it you? Even with vital issues at stake, not everyone arrives in a state of readiness. Some people rely on past experience, expecting to use their wits and develop a strategy as they go. As an example, a manager in a manufacturing company had to negotiate with a union. He thought all they needed to agree on were salaries and insurance benefits. Then the union representative raised issues related to job safety and scheduling.

The manager wasn't prepared. He didn't have all the data he needed and was caught off guard. He ended up agreeing to some things that weren't necessarily in his company's best interest.

Preparation is the foundation that win-win solutions are built on. In this case, the manager learned the hard way that much of a negotiation's success – or failure – takes place before the parties ever sit down.

There's no such thing as being overprepared for a negotiation. Preparation is not just important to achieving your desired goals – it's also key to determining what your goals are.

After all, negotiation is the process by which opposing sides reach agreement through discussion and compromise. Differences are resolved by bargaining to reach a mutually acceptable agreement. So it's clear that for a successful outcome, you need to prepare by considering what you want, as well as what the other party wants. When you know as much as possible about all the issues on the negotiating table, you'll be able to articulate your arguments, prevent surprises, and have immediate responses.

Many benefits arise from being prepared for a negotiation:
- you'll have better control of outcomes, because you'll be more confident,
- you'll have a better understanding of the other party, which will make the negotiation easier, and
- you'll be able to craft the best solution possible – with fewer modifications later on – because your requirements, and those of the other party, are well defined.

The time you spend on investigative work will vary, depending on the kind of negotiation. There's no minimum or maximum time range that will apply to all negotiation preparations.

You may have to become an expert in something you previously knew nothing about, learn about legal ramifications or governmental regulations, or delve into background information about the company on the other side of the table.

But the time you spend in preparation for the negotiation is an investment. It can shorten the negotiations and allow for better understanding between you and your counterpart, making the negotiations easier.

IDENTIFYING WHAT YOU WANT

Identifying what you want
There are five key considerations in preparing for negotiations: your overall goal; your needs, wants, and expectations; the needs, wants, and expectations of the other party; the issues of the situation; and the type of relationship you have with the other party. You can group the preparation considerations under two headings: identifying what you want and gathering information on the context of the negotiation.

Perhaps you have firsthand knowledge of negotiation failures. Or maybe you thought of a union strike, such as one in a school district.

In one real-life example, more than 90% of teachers rejected what their school board called its "last, best, and final offer." Even with experienced mediation negotiators, talks broke down and a strike occurred.

And in an example from the retail manufacturing industry, the Purchasing Department of a giant department store chain squeezed a small supplier to decrease its selling price to the point where there was no profit left in the contract. The supplier had no incentive to provide a quality product, and, ultimately, customers complained. In this case, no one was the winner of the negotiation.

To help avoid negotiation failures, the first step is to identify what you want. After all, you need to know what your target is in a negotiation before you can do any other planning. To accomplish this, you need to identify your overall goal and your needs, wants, and expectations. Identifying what you want will also help you determine what tactics to use. It's also important to make sure everyone working on your negotiation team is in agreement about the aims.

Your overall goal

To determine an overall goal, you begin by identifying your ideal outcome. Ask yourself questions such as "What do I really want?", "What am I willing to compromise?", and "What can I afford to lose?"

A goal is a realistic target where expectations are set by using an objective standard. Asking these questions help you identify your goal.

A bottom line is different. It's the bare minimum that you can agree to – the point below which you walk away. Below the bottom line, you could achieve more by not negotiating at all, or by waiting for another opportunity.

Your needs, wants, and expectations

Think of your needs, wants, and expectations as your wish list. Consider everything you want, need, or expect to happen as a result of the negotiation. Try to differentiate between what you want to have happen and what you really need to occur.

For example, you might want to pay a new employee a salary at the low end of the scale. But what if that person has to work in a location with a very high cost of living? When you need to factor in the costs associated with working in an expensive location, you shouldn't expect to find a candidate who is willing to work for a low salary.

Identifying your goal and your needs, wants, and expectations will help you figure out the best strategies and tactics to use.

For example, is your primary goal to win at any cost? Or do you want the best deal that still maintains the integrity of your relationship with the other party? The answers will provide a framework for your negotiation strategy.

A benefit of having definite objectives in mind before setting out to negotiate is that you'll be able to better control the outcome. And when your goal is more realistic and reasonable, there's a greater likelihood you'll achieve it.

After you've come up with your "wish list" of wants, needs, and expectations, you'll have to prioritize it. Sorting your list into categories will help you determine what concessions you can make when the negotiation is underway. Must-have items are those that are vital to the negotiation's success. Nice-to-

have items add value, but aren't as important. Would-like-to-have-but-can-live-without items are those things that aren't deal breakers. If you have to make concessions, these are the items you put on the table first.

Must have

For example, if you're the hiring manager at a legal firm that specializes in environmental law, a must-have requirement when negotiating to hire a new lawyer is experience in the area. You may find an otherwise perfect applicant, with the right salary needs, attitude, and credentials. But a lack of experience in environmental law will be a deal breaker.

Nice to have

Say you're in charge of negotiating a contract for new computers for your entire software company. You decide a 24-hour repair service would be nice to have. It's not vitally important for a 9-to-5 business with skilled computer personnel on staff, but you'd like it, as your software engineers work flexible hours.

Now, if you worked for a hospital and were negotiating the same type of contract, a 24-hour repair service could easily be a must-have requirement.

Would like to have, but can live without

If you're negotiating with your manager about getting more training, you might decide that you'd like to go on a week-long intensive seminar that's located a few hundred miles away. You could settle for a short course that is located closer to home. The longer seminar falls into the category of something you'd like to have, but can live without.

If you make a concession on the seminar, you can get the training you need while demonstrating your willingness to meet your manager halfway.

Question

When preparing for a negotiation, what should you do to help you identify what you want out of the negotiation?

Options:

1. Clarify what your best deal would be

2. Brainstorm all of the issues that affect your side of the deal and decide which are most important

3. Prepare yourself for not getting everything you need

4. Place what you can most afford to lose at the top of your priority list

Answer

Option 1: This is a correct option. One step in planning is to ask yourself what you really want – what your overall goal is. If you have definite objectives in mind before setting out to negotiate, you'll be better able to stay on track.

Option 2: This is a correct option. Your needs, wants, and expectations of everything to do with the negotiation need to be identified and prioritized so you stay in control and get a good result.

Option 3: This option is incorrect. You shouldn't have to prepare yourself for failure if you have planned well and prioritized your wants, needs, and expectations.

Option 4: This option is incorrect. What you can most afford to lose are items you might like to have, but can live without. Therefore, they are at the bottom of the priority list and can readily be used as bargaining chips.

GATHERING INFORMATION

Gathering information

Knowing what you want from a negotiation is only part of being prepared. It's hard enough to figure out what you need from a negotiation – understanding someone else's interests is even more difficult. It's human nature to want to make assumptions about the other side's goals, but try not to jump to any conclusions.

For example, if you're about to enter negotiations to acquire a small family-owned company, you might assume the sellers' main goal is to get as high a purchase price as possible. While you might be right, be sure you're not basing your strategy on guesswork.

Gather information that allows you to uncover what's really going on. Perhaps the sellers have to sell the company to settle probate or another legal matter, and speed is as important a goal as price. Or maybe the owners want to retire, but can take time to find a buyer who'll take good care of the business and its employees.

Your negotiation strategy would be different for each negotiating scenario.

No matter what the negotiation, gathering information about it means considering: the needs, wants, and expectations of the other party; the issues surrounding the situation; and the type of relationship you have with the other party. With a better understanding of the other side, you'll be more confident at the negotiating table, and the negotiation strategy will need fewer modifications because the requirements of both sides will be well defined.

Some negotiators think it's just too hard to figure out what the other side wants. Their strategy is to focus on their own needs, and let the other side worry about itself.

But such an attitude can lead to any number of undesirable outcomes, from a failure to agree to a breakdown of the relationship, or even an outright conflict.

Understand the other party's needs and motivations and work with them as much as you can. Only then will you build rapport and negotiate in an environment of cooperation.

Useful questions to ask yourself:

There are many different questions that you might ask yourself when gathering information on the other party. Here are some key questions you might want to consider, if you haven't already.

– Are there definite outcomes the other side must achieve?

– Are there any relationship goals they want to achieve?

– How critical is this negotiation to their company?

– Who are the individuals doing the negotiation? Are they experienced negotiators or novices? Are they aggressive or do they avoid conflict?

You need to get specific information about the issues surrounding a negotiation. For instance, you need to know if the other party has a deadline, what the other company has done before in this situation, and what the current trends in the marketplace are. Specific issues that frequently arise in negotiations include details about price, volume, time, and quality.

Price

Money is the most popular negotiation issue. Price determination are often a critical part of the process. Figuring out your selling or buying amount is best done in advance.

For example, if you're trying to buy a new and innovative electronic device for your large department store, you need to establish exactly how low you can go before the other side will decide their profit margin is too low and walk away.

Volume

Suppose you're a salesperson negotiating the sale of products based on the amount ordered. Will your deal-making include discount offers? What consideration will you give to the buyer for larger-volume purchases?

Time

Matters concerning time are always critical, especially since deadlines often drive the deal. Be clear about your willingness to give up something – perhaps a feature or level of quality – to meet a deadline. The price you agreed to pay may not be worth the effort.

Quality

Imagine that you recently purchased an expensive security system for your office. What happens if you're unsatisfied with it? Protect your investment in advance by finding out the seller's policy regarding exchanges, replacements, warranty, and refunds.

In addition to knowing about issues such as price, quality, and time, you also need information about the nature of the relationship you share with the other party. The approach you take in the negotiation – for instance, whether you're more competitive or more compromising – is based in large part on this relationship. Is this a one-time encounter, or will you be dealing long term? How important is the relationship to each business?

Most negotiations take place with people you need to keep working with, even after the negotiation is over. To explore the true relationship between negotiating parties, avoid assumptions and focus on both parties' interests in several areas:

- Discover what influences the other party. What kind of values and market drivers does the other side have, and are they the same in your company?
- Investigate if there are any difficult matters between you and the other party. Are there any areas where coming to an agreement will be exceptionally difficult?
- Consider whether there are unresolved problems that will foster a competitive emotional environment, which is bad for collaboration and bad for a successful outcome to a negotiation. How has the relationship been historically? If you encounter an old problem, plan a way to close off that problem.

When you gather information about the other party, make sure you find the right information for a particular negotiation. For example, Hugo is a manager who needs to talk to other managers about reducing the number of meetings he has to attend.

Hugo needs to find out what the other managers need and expect out of the meetings he attends. Perhaps they're looking for him to back them up in sticky situations, or perhaps they want to be kept updated on the status of his projects. Hugo needs details on these kinds of issues.

Hugo also needs to think about the relationship he has with the other managers. For example, one manager, with whom Hugo works closely, may rely on regular meetings for timely updates that help him meet key company goals. Another manager, who relies less on Hugo's work, may be scheduling meetings because she prefers face-to-face encounters.

In the end, when you prepare properly for a negotiation – finding out all you can about the other party and the issues at stake, as well as clarifying your own needs and expectations – you'll know how to get the other side not only to agree to the deal you need, but to be happy with it.

Question

If you enter into a negotiation fully prepared, what benefits might you realize?

Options:

1. You'll have a better control of outcomes
2. You'll have an easier time in the negotiations
3. You'll be able to craft the best solution possible
4. You'll be able to fully control the negotiation
5. You'll always be able to get your own way in the negotiation

Answer

Option 1: This is a correct option. If you're prepared, you'll have better control of outcomes because you'll be more confident.

Option 2: This is a correct option. Negotiations are easier when you have a better understanding of the other party, which comes from being prepared.

Option 3: This is a correct option. Preparation will help you craft a solution that achieves your goal without destroying working relationships.

Option 4: This option is incorrect. Full control of the negotiation is not a benefit of the preparation stage, and isn't possible in any case. Part of your negotiations will be a give-and-take with the other side.

Option 5: This option is incorrect. If you got your own way above all else, you'd most likely be manipulating, not negotiating.

Question

When preparing for a negotiation, what kind of information should you gather about the other party and the context of the negotiation?

Options:

1. Identify what the other party thinks will happen as the result of the negotiation

2. Find out specifics about the other side's interests, background, and reputation

3. Consider whether or not this negotiation is the first of many you'll have with the other party

4. Find out the information you need in the first half-hour of the negotiation session

5. Focus on negative information about the other party so that you can use it to make them agree to your position

6. Get details on issues such as deadlines, the company's experience in similar negotiations, and trends in the market

Answer

Option 1: This is a correct option. Gathering information includes determining the needs, wants, and expectations of the other party.

Option 2: This is a correct option. To determine the specifics of the context of the negotiation, you need to find out everything you can about the other side's situation.

Option 3: This is a correct option. The type of relationship you have with the other party is of vital importance in determining a negotiation strategy.

Option 4: This option is incorrect. Although you'll discover information as you negotiate, you still need to prepare by gathering information about the other party and about issues surrounding the negotiation.

Option 5: This option is incorrect. Focusing on negative information and then using it against the other party could result in conflict and put an end to the negotiations. The focus should be on finding information that enables you to cooperate with the other party.

Option 6: This option is correct. You need to get specific information on issues surrounding the negotiation. Often, details related to price, volume, time, and quality are important to uncover.

SECTION 2 - PREPARE FOR COMPROMISES IN A NEGOTIATION

SECTION 2 - Prepare for Compromises in a Negotiation

Negotiations are all about give and take. To be truly prepared for a negotiation, you have to prepare for compromise and plan for it to happen.

The first step is to identify what would be good outcomes for both sides. Then you identify how to create value through trades. That will lead you to outcomes that are mutually agreeable.

CONSIDERING GOOD OUTCOMES

Considering good outcomes

If you've ever had a confrontational or unpleasant experience in a negotiation, you're not alone. Many people go through this on a personal level if they buy or sell a house, or if they go through a divorce, for example. When members of the other side think they won't have to deal with you ever again – and therefore don't need your goodwill – they sometimes feel it's OK to win a negotiation while you lose out. But it doesn't have to be that way.

Compromise is what leads to win-win situations that don't damage trust, reputation, or teamwork. Compromise works.

After all, people use compromise as a tool all the time. In the real world, no one gets absolutely everything they ask for, and it's no different in negotiations. There has to be give and take from both sides. But you have to avoid giving up too much, or giving in on the wrong issues.

Benefits of preparing for compromise

Sorin Dumitrascu

With adequate preparation and time to determine your "must have," "nice to have," and "would like to have, but can live without" areas, you won't be forced into making a sudden decision you might regret later. Only with preparation will you be able to determine a range of acceptable settlement options for a negotiation.

Once you reach the stage of preparing for compromises in a negotiation, you have a good idea of what each side wants. But you still need to determine how the information you've gathered will work or fit together in the negotiation. It helps to have already prioritized your wants and needs. But you should still plan how far you can compromise your demands.

Two steps can help you prepare for likely negotiation compromises:

- Consider what the possible good outcomes would be for both you and the other side. Ideally, you'll be able to create a win-win situation.
- Identify how to create value through trades. In an ideal situation, the other party will want what you're prepared to trade.

Even if it initially appears the two sides are opposed, the other party may just have different goals from the ones you expect. That's why considering the best outcomes is the first step. To do this, you draw on the priorities you previously mapped, as well as what you've determined to be the interests of the other party. As an example, consider Rita. She's an accountant who needs to talk to her boss Stefan about taking a leave of absence to care for her mother, who has Alzheimer's.

Determining each side's interests is sometimes difficult, since it's not always easy to find out what they're thinking.

Rita

Rita thinks that taking an unpaid leave of absence – as provided for in her company's HR policy – is the only way to achieve her goals. Her ideal terms would allow her flexibility enough to take her mother to her many doctor's appointments. Rita would also like to be home by 4:00 p.m., when the adult day program is over. She'd prefer to be able to maintain her income, but she doesn't see any way to do that.

Stefan

Stefan's ideal outcome would be to have no changes at all. Rita is an excellent employee, and he needs her output to make his production numbers. But he knows that Rita is allowed to take a leave of absence under company policy.

Question

Do you think Rita taking an unpaid leave is the best possible outcome for either side of this negotiation?

Options:

1. Yes
2. No

Answer

Even for Rita, an unpaid leave isn't the best option because it leaves her without income. There are several other feasible alternatives that would allow both Rita and Stefan to attain most, if not all, of their goals.

An unpaid leave of absence isn't the only possible option. To prepare for her negotiation with Stefan, Rita should determine what she truly needs, and not just settle for what she thinks she can get.

And on the other side, even though it might be easier for him, Stefan can't just deny Rita's request completely.

After all, the company does have a leave policy, and Rita's circumstances do fit its requirements.

If Stefan did turn down her request, Rita might even quit, which would create a much bigger problem for both of them.

But if Stefan prepares well for his negotiation with Rita, he could learn what her key issue is. He needs to understand that she needs more job schedule flexibility. Then he could come up with workable outcomes that allow his department to still reach its production goals, and allow Rita to take care of her mother.

CREATING VALUE THROUGH TRADES

Creating value through trades
Once you know what a good outcome would be – for both your side and the other party's side – the next step in preparing for likely compromises is finding valuable trades. You need to identify areas of agreement and potential compromise, as well as trading opportunities. In compromise, neither side gets all they want, but they make concessions to achieve a mutually acceptable agreement. Trades ensure each of the parties in the negotiation gets something it wants in return for something it values less.

In the trading step of negotiation preparation, keep in mind what you need, what you want, and what you can afford to lose.

Consider objections to your outcomes from the other party and how you might respond to them, along with any possible compromises or concessions.

The most important thing you should be looking for are differences – differences between the way you prioritize wants and needs and the way the other party prioritizes them. These prioritization differences are what help create a win-win outcome.

Think for a moment about your own negotiations – perhaps with customers, suppliers, or fellow employees. Are you pulling and tugging with each other in a win-lose framework?

For a negotiation to be win-win, both parties should end up feeling positive, which helps maintain good working relationships.

When considering trades, ask yourself what you and the other side each have that the other wants. What would you be comfortable giving away?

Sometimes a little creative thinking can identify areas that have little value to you, but more to the other party. Consider ways you could satisfy the other side with something costing you very little. Remember, though, that if you're giving value, you should ask for something in return. Depending on your industry and the issues to be negotiated, possible areas to investigate include delivery schedules or production deadlines, technical support or repair services, and office space or machinery and equipment.

Schedules and deadlines

When it comes to schedules and deadlines, the side of the negotiation table you're on makes a big difference.

For a customer, having purchase deliveries spread out over the course of a month might be of no great consequence. But for a supplier with strained production facilities, it may be very important and have real value in trading.

Support services

Support services such as technical support or installation and repair services can have high or low value, depending on the situation.

A customer might find great value in being offered three months of free repair services if needed. But for a vendor – especially one with confidence in quality products – free service is nothing of consequence. Even if the service is needed, the vendor incurs little cost.

Space and equipment

Office space, machinery, or other equipment can be useful, low-cost areas to trade value. For example, another department in your company might find great value in the offer of one or two high-powered workstations that your people rarely use. That department may be able to offer you something in exchange that you value more than it does.

Remember Rita and Stefan? Stefan might have assumed Rita wanted a total leave of absence, but he kept an open mind and found out she'd really rather work and maintain at least a partial income.

As part of his negotiation preparation, Stefan asked himself what a good outcome would be for Rita. He discovered that what she needs, above all, is the flexibility to take her mother to appointments and be home by 4:00 p.m. when the adult day program ends.

So Stefan is looking for trading opportunities. He doesn't want to lose Rita as an employee, but he has production goals to meet and he doesn't want to overwork his other employees.

Question

What do you think are the best options for Stefan to offer Rita in order to create value through trades?

Options:
1. Rita could work reduced hours – with a reduced salary – so she'd be home by 4:00 p.m., and Stefan could use the salary reduction to hire a part-time intern
2. Rita could work from home most days, making sure she gives Stefan a scheduled plan for her work to be delivered
3. Rita could keep her current salary and work a reduced schedule from home, taking time off for her mother's doctor's appointments
4. Rita could schedule all her necessary onsite meetings in the mornings and work from home in the afternoons
5. Rita could work four ten-hour days and have three-day weekends

Answer

Option 1: This is a correct option. Rita won't lose significant income and will be able to care for her mother the way she'd like. And Stefan will still have all of Rita's hours covered.

Option 2: This is a correct option. For an employee, the opportunity to work from home can produce great satisfaction while costing the employer nothing. Stefan would keep the full-time worker he needs – with a plan for Rita to follow – and Rita can care for her mother and keep her income.

Option 3: This is an incorrect option. Working a reduced schedule and taking more time off means Stefan is making all the concessions. He's not asking for anything in trade, and Rita is getting all the value.

Option 4: This is a correct option. With this schedule, Rita can attend meetings in the morning while her mother is at the adult day program and still be home by 4:00 p.m.

And Stefan won't lose any hours or have to hire someone new.

Option 5: This is an incorrect option. While working four ten-hour days is a different schedule than Rita works now, it's not going to get her home by 4:00 p.m. Stefan isn't offering the kind of flexibility that Rita needs.

As Stefan and Rita find out, sometimes flexibility can be more important than money. Stefan could offer Rita several alternatives that are better for both of them than her initial request for unpaid leave.

More than one of the options would have her at home when needed and still let her have most – or even all – of her income. And they wouldn't cause problems for Stefan or the department.

This negotiation creates value for both sides.

Remember, planning your outcomes beforehand helps you avoid getting caught up in competition and emotion once the negotiation has begun. After all, the goal of a negotiation is to satisfy your interests, not to win at all costs. Identifying areas of compromise and potential trades gives you the flexibility to seek out win-win solutions.

Question

Oralia is a hospital administrator who's selling an X-ray machine to make room for a new digital unit. Taku wants to buy the machine, but is trying to get it for an amount much lower than Oralia's asking price. He wants to make as quick a purchase as possible because his small clinic needs the machine.

How should Oralia prepare for compromises in this negotiation?

Options:

1. Oralia should consider that Taku would like to buy the X-ray machine at a low price, but that she needs to get the appraised value

2. Oralia could offer a lease-to-own financing contract at the original purchase price, which would save Taku interest costs

3. Oralia should rehearse how she will decline the offer without making Taku defensive

4. Oralia should consider that Taku needs the machine and insist that he pay the full price she is offering

Answer

Option 1: This is a correct option. Oralia is considering good outcomes for both sides, which will help her identify areas of compromise.

Option 2: This is a correct option. Oralia is identifying how to create value through trades. In this case, she would get the price she needs and Taku would still come out ahead financially.

Option 3: This is an incorrect option. Oralia is not considering what the best outcome for Taku would be or how she might trade value. Instead, she is focusing on what to say to decline his offer.

Option 4: This is an incorrect option. Oralia should consider what a good outcome would be for Taku as well as the hospital. If she goes into the negotiation with this approach, it could lead to both parties losing.

SECTION 3 - KNOW YOUR BATNA AND "WALK AWAY" POINT IN A NEGOTIATION

SECTION 3 - Know Your BATNA and "Walk Away" Point in a Negotiation

The acronym BATNA stands for best alternative to a negotiated agreement, and it's what you have in reserve if you don't reach an agreement in a negotiation. To strengthen your position in a negotiation, you can improve your BATNA, identify the other side's BATNA, or weaken their BATNA.

The BATNA is also used to help determine your walk away point in a negotiation, which is the point at which you reach an impasse and can't agree. Knowing your walk away point before you begin will help you determine if a zone of possible agreement – or ZOPA – exists. If there is a ZOPA, you may be able to come to an agreement that benefits both sides more than any alternative options would.

IDENTIFYING YOUR BATNA

Identifying your BATNA

What would you do if you failed to reach an agreement in a negotiation? After all, you may find all proposals unacceptable, and even compromise can fail. You don't want to end up with a bad deal, or no deal at all, and you don't want to waste all the time, energy, and effort you've put into planning a negotiation. What you need is a safety net.

Your safety net is called a BATNA, a concept developed by Roger Fisher and William Ury of the Harvard Negotiation Project.

The acronym stands for the best alternative to a negotiated agreement, and it's the preferred course of action in the absence of a deal.

Having a BATNA means knowing what you'll do – and how much it will cost you – if you can't come to an agreement with the other side. If you don't know your BATNA before entering a negotiation, you won't know whether a deal makes sense, or when to walk away.

Listing all of your possible alternatives to a negotiated agreement is an important part of negotiation preparation.

Knowing your BATNA gives you strength, confidence, and clarity. Your walk-away alternatives give you power to get what you want – the more easily you can walk away from a negotiation, the more influence you have during the process. A confident attitude compels others to listen and to realize that they have to meet your interests if they want your agreement. And clarity comes from having a realistic view of the alternatives that are viable options to reaching agreement.

Your BATNA will vary, depending on what industry you're in and what side of the negotiating table you're on.

Purchasing

If you're negotiating a deal with a supplier, your BATNA can be the ability to walk away and buy from an alternative seller.

Or if you've received a shipment of items that aren't up to your quality standards and are getting no satisfaction from the supplier, your BATNA is the next dispute resolution step in your contract – whether it's mediation, arbitration, or going to court.

Consulting

If you're a consultant negotiating with a potential client about an assignment, money is always going to be part of the agreement.

Your BATNA might be another job you have lined up – perhaps one with a flexible schedule that you can move up if current negotiations fail.

Banking

Perhaps you're a CFO who's planning to approach your bank for a loan. You need the bank to agree to give your company the loan at a good interest rate.

Your BATNA could be to have researched all the other financial institutions with good interest rates who'd lend you the money.

A strong BATNA puts you in a good position to negotiate for more favorable terms. You know you can fall back on an alternative that's as good – or better than – what you're negotiating for. A weak BATNA, however, gives you little power to negotiate – especially if the other side knows your position. With a weak BATNA – or if you don't know what your BATNA is at all – you'll have a hard time walking away from a proposal, even if it's not that great.

For example, Amrit is a self-employed technical writer who's negotiating for a month-long contract. She has another contract available to her, which would allow her to spend that month on other billable work. That gives her a fairly strong BATNA.

If, however, Amrit had no other work lined up, her only alternative might be sitting around waiting for the phone to ring. And that's a very weak BATNA.

Consider Katerina, an HR manager for a package delivery service. Katerina wants to hire Omar, a civil engineer, for an open position in the Logistics Department. Her BATNA isn't very strong, but a weak BATNA isn't the end of the story.

You can strengthen a BATNA – and with it, a negotiating position – using three different techniques.

Improve your BATNA

To improve your BATNA, brainstorm and research any options available to you if the negotiation fails. Anything that improves your BATNA strengthens your position.

Consider bringing third parties into the mix, making your BATNA more achievable and viable. For instance, having more than one alternate vendor – or job candidate, as in Katerina's case – willing to satisfy supply needs can strengthen a BATNA.

Katerina has a few other candidates for the logistics position, but Omar was recently downsized from the exact same position at her firm's only major competitor. He is by far the best candidate, and he knows it.

Katerina could research who else was laid off in the same department, and invite them to apply for the job. She could also consider that the job could be done via telecommuting, which would allow her to expand her pool of applicants.

And finally, she could always hire a less experienced person for a much smaller salary. All these options would strengthen her BATNA.

Identify the other side's BATNA

A good estimation of the other side's BATNA is a source of negotiation strength. When you know the other negotiators' alternatives, you know how far you can go before they walk away.

To learn the other side's most likely alternatives, research the viable options. Consult company reports, contact networked sources, and identify the other party's strategic goals.

You may find the other side is overestimating its BATNA, which will strengthen your position. Or maybe the other party's alternative to a deal may be strong relative to yours. Either way, knowing in advance gives you time to prepare for a more favorable outcome.

Katerina does a little investigating and finds that Omar's BATNA is quite strong. He's already been offered another job.

The other company is a start-up, and Katerina has heard through the grapevine that salaries aren't as competitive. Knowing Omar's alternative in advance gives Katerina the chance to emphasize salary in her job offer.

Weaken the other side's BATNA

Anything that weakens the other side's BATNA gives the negotiation a whole new slant. In some cases, you can weaken the other side's BATNA directly by injecting a new element. In other cases, you can make a BATNA appear to be less attractive.

In the retail world, it's common for sellers to try to weaken a buyer's BATNA using "buy now" sales. They inject the element of time into a standard price negotiation, and try to make you believe you have no alternatives to an immediate purchase.

You may panic and buy based on this perception, when in fact there may be another sale in a month's time, or you may get a similar product from a different seller, or you might not need the item at all.

Katerina knows Omar has had a job offer from a start-up company, and that he's the best candidate for her position. What can she do to weaken his BATNA?

Katerina can bring up the fact that in start-up companies, the pay isn't as competitive and the hours are longer. There's also less security than with a well-established company.

She can also point out that her company's signing bonus is in the form of cash, not potentially valueless stock that won't vest for five years. She weakens Omar's BATNA directly by offering more money and indirectly by pointing out its flaws.

Now consider the situation from Omar's viewpoint. He has been offered a position at another company, although at a lower salary than he'd like.

Improve your BATNA

To improve his BATNA, Omar point outs that the start-up company has more flexible hours than Katerina's company.

He also researches comparable jobs to back up his expectations about salary and benefits.

Identify the other side's BATNA

Because Omar is very good at networking, he keeps in touch with his laid-off former coworkers. He can easily identify Katerina's BATNA.

Several of his coworkers are still job hunting and would be acceptable alternatives for this position. But Omar knows they don't have his particular combination of education and experience in logistics.

Weaken the other side's BATNA

To weaken Katerina's BATNA, Omar reads her company's web site and makes note of the fact that the corporate goals are to become more lean and logistically efficient.

Omar can use this information to emphasize his strengths in logistical efficiency and the differences between him and his former coworkers in this area.

Question

You go to a supplier to buy some badly needed parts to complete a project. The supplier senses your urgency. You want the lowest price possible, while he wants the highest price.

How can you use a BATNA to help strengthen your negotiating position?

Options:

1. Before negotiating on price, you find other suppliers who can handle your order

2. You discover that a competitor placed a big order with the same supplier for the same part

3. You know that even though the supplier has an alternate customer for the same part, that customer is in a precarious financial state

4. You decide you're willing to pay a higher price since you need the parts now

5. You discover that a competitor ordered the same part from the same supplier, and decide to outbid

Answer

Option 1: This is a correct option. You'll improve your BATNA if you have several good alternatives to this supplier.

Option 2: This is a correct option. If the supplier has another customer for the same items, you've identified a strong BATNA and can plan for it.

Option 3: This is a correct option. You can weaken the supplier's BATNA by highlighting the news, recently made public, about the alternate customer's financial state.

Option 4: This option is incorrect. If you allow for concessions under the pressure of deadlines, you're not even trying to improve your BATNA.

Option 5: This option is incorrect. Deciding to get in a bidding war with a competitor will only strengthen the supplier's BATNA, not yours.

DETERMINING THE WALK AWAY POINT

Determining the walk away point

BATNAs give you a standard for determining when to end a negotiation. But when preparing for a negotiation, you also need to know your "walk away" point, which is your bottom line or reservation price. This is the least favorable point at which you will still accept a deal. It's where you draw the line.

If your negotiation comes to an impasse, your BATNA is what comes next. But your walk away point is the most you'll give – or the least you'll take – while still coming to agreement.

Your walk away point is derived from your BATNA, but it's not the same. The walk away point is still just inside an active negotiation, while the BATNA is outside it.

If a deal is only about money, and a certain dollar offer is what you can get as an alternative to the negotiation, then your walk away point may be equal to your BATNA. Suppose you want to buy a yellow car that's advertised for

$20,000. But the same make and model car in a different color is being sold elsewhere for $18,000. Your walk away point when negotiating for the yellow car is $18,000, and it's also your BATNA.

Consider this example. You're the CEO of a large coffee shop chain. You currently pay $2 per pound for premium coffee beans. The quality is good and it's a fair price, but you're thinking about switching to free-trade organic beans. While your customer base won't balk at a small price increase, you can't pay more than $3 per pound without pricing yourself out of the market. Before you enter into a negotiation with your supplier, you need to determine your walk away point and your BATNA.

BATNA

Your best alternative if the negotiations fail is to keep on doing what you're doing and not switch to a more expensive coffee.

Alternatively, you can research other suppliers and coffee cooperatives, but your fall-back BATNA is always going to be the current price you pay for beans: $2 per pound.

Walk away point

In this case, your bottom line is different from your BATNA price of $2 per pound for the old beans. You're willing to pay up to $3 per pound for free-trade, organic coffee beans, so that's your walk away point.

The new beans have different characteristics that make them more attractive than the ones you're currently using. So you're willing to pay more for them. But if you can't get them for under $3 per pound, you'll walk away and stay with your BATNA.

Question

Colleen is attempting to negotiate a flexible work schedule that enables her to work from home. She ideally wants to be able to work from home every day – five days a week – but is willing to start with just one if she has to. Her boss would rather not allow it at all, but is willing to consider letting Colleen work up to two days from home.

What is Colleen's walk away point?

Options:
1. One day
2. Two days
3. Five days
4. Finding another job

Answer

Option 1: This is the correct option. One day is Colleen's minimum, so it's her walk away point. If she doesn't get that, she'll choose her BATNA.

Option 2: This option is incorrect. Two days is the upper limit of Colleen's boss's range; it's not the point at which Colleen will walk away.

Option 3: This option is incorrect. Five days is Colleen's ideal. But five days isn't her bottom line, and she won't walk away if she doesn't get all five.

Option 4: This option is incorrect. Finding another position is Colleen's BATNA if she's so set on changing her schedule that she'll quit. But it's not her walk away point.

IDENTIFYING THE ZOPA

Identifying the ZOPA

So what happens now? Suppose you know the walk away points and the ideal outcomes of both parties in a negotiation. The difference between those points is the range of expectations each side has. When there's overlap between the two ranges, there's an area of common ground. This area is known as the zone of possible agreement, or ZOPA.

Each party's walk away point determines one end of the ZOPA. Whether people are selling products, ideas, or services, they're usually trying to get the best price possible. But there's always going to be a bottom line.

Buyers want to pay the least amount possible, but there's usually a higher amount they're prepared to pay. But that maximum amount is a point they won't go over. If a ZOPA exists, it's in the overlap between these high and low limits. The ZOPA is the area or range in which a deal that satisfies both parties can take place.

Remember, though, that the letter P in ZOPA stands for "possible." There's not always going to be a zone of overlap in the ranges of the seller and buyer. And even when a ZOPA exists, there are no guarantees. The negotiation may still fail if the parties are unable to agree. Having a ZOPA means an agreement is more likely to occur, but it's not definite.

Consider this example. A company needs to sell its fleet of delivery vans. Rico, a manager, advertises the vans for $40,000. While $40,000 is the optimum value, Rico can let the vans go for as low as $35,000. Raj is interested, but can only afford to pay $37,000. He makes a first offer of $34,000. Neither Rico nor Raj know the other's bottom line. The ZOPA is from $35,000 to $37,000. In this comfort area, Rico and Raj might be able to agree.

Question

Remember Colleen? She wants to work from home five days a week, but is willing to start with one. Her boss doesn't want any changes, but is considering letting Colleen work up to two days from home.

What is the zone of possible agreement for this negotiation?

Options:
1. 1-2 days
2. 0-1 day
3. 1-5 days
4. 2-5 days
5. There is no ZOPA

Answer

Option 1: This is the correct option. Colleen's walk away point is one day and her boss's is two days. The area between these points is the ZOPA.

Option 2: This option is incorrect. Zero days is below Colleen's walk away point of one day, so there is no overlap at zero days.

Option 3: This option is incorrect. Between one and five days is Colleen's total settlement range. But her boss won't go above two days, so there's no overlap up to five days.

Option 4: This option is incorrect. Colleen's boss's walk away point is two days at the most, so there's no overlap between two and five days.

Option 5: This option is incorrect. There is a zone of agreement between Colleen's bottom line and her boss's walk away point.

CHAPTER 3 - COMMUNICATING

CHAPTER 3 - Communicating
   SECTION 1 - <u>Setting the Tone for a Negotiation Session</u>
   SECTION 2 - <u>Making a Proposal in a Negotiation</u>
   SECTION 3 - <u>Responding to the Other Party in a Negotiation</u>

SECTION 1 - SETTING THE TONE FOR A NEGOTIATION SESSION

SECTION 1 - Setting the Tone for a Negotiation Session

Although a confrontational approach may occasionally be appropriate for a particular negotiation, most often you will want to create a collaborative tone. This means you focus on a win-win outcome – one that allows both you and the other party to walk away feeling as though you've received enough of what you set out to get.

To establish this sort of tone, you can use specific strategies such as building rapport with the other negotiator, staying focused on the positives, and remaining consistent throughout the negotiation to build trust and credibility.

THE IMPORTANCE OF TONE

The importance of tone

Negotiations can be big or small. They may be business related or personal, and may include different cultural and international considerations. But in all cases, the tone set at the start of the negotiation is critical to achieving a successful outcome.

The way you conduct negotiations may vary, ranging from a confrontational approach to a collaborative one. Although each approach has advantages and disadvantages, setting a collaborative tone is almost always better because it focuses attention on the need to reach a mutually acceptable solution.

Confrontational approaches consider the negotiation a win-or-lose contest between two parties.

Professional sports, for example, are confrontational. Winning means the other person or team must lose. The most the loser can hope for is a pat on the back and the promise of a future opportunity to get even.

When you use a confrontational approach like this in business negotiations, however, you can damage future relationships. You may successfully negotiate a high rate of pay, but do you really want your new employer to feel like she has paid too much for your services? Or if you're a buyer, do you want to bully your way to a bargain that makes your suppliers think they won't make any money dealing with you?

But in most business negotiations, you'll have a continuing relationship with the other party, so trying to meet that person's needs is important.

In a negotiation, winning what you need doesn't necessarily mean the other party has to lose. It doesn't have to be about getting the most you can, no matter what. It's often better in the long run if the other negotiating party walks away thinking they got what they wanted as well.

Achieving this sort of win-win outcome requires a collaborative, problem-solving approach to negotiation rather than a confrontational one.

Collaboration involves setting aside personal feelings about winning or losing and focusing on resolving the joint issue. Working together, you hope to reach a mutually satisfactory agreement, with the emphasis on obtaining your objectives rather than scoring points or beating down your opponent. Setting a collaborative tone begins with building rapport with the other person, focusing on the positive aspects of the negotiation, and being consistent so that you build trust and confidence in the relationship.

Build rapport

Building rapport is a way to increase understanding, make communication more effective, and get better results. This involves creating a connection between you and the other party in the negotiation, which will give you both a better sense of the other person's manner and feelings. When you build rapport, information is exchanged in a natural, effortless, and efficient way.

Focus on the positive aspects

It's important to look at the positive aspects of the negotiation, such as the things you have in common, your confidence in your negotiation's eventual success, and your willingness to work together to reach a mutually satisfying outcome. Negotiating in a positive manner keeps things moving forward.

Be consistent

Consistency builds trust over time. If you start out friendly, flexible, and casual but switch to an aggressive, take-it-or-leave-it attitude part way into the negotiation, your negotiating opponent will be confused and unsure of you. Likewise, starting out aggressively and then backpeddling and being conciliatory will destroy trust.

BUILDING RAPPORT

Building rapport

Hannah, an experienced negotiator, works for a real estate development firm that's building a new shopping mall. She's already met with Jose, the head of the town's planning commission, but they're about to sit down to negotiate the details of the development proposal. Follow along as Hannah tries to set an appropriate tone for the negotiation.

Hannah: Good to see you again Jose. I understand you're just back from a trip to the Caribbean. Did you have a good time?

Jose: Yes, it was great to get away to a nice warm climate and lie around on the beach for a week. I'm feeling refreshed and ready to get back to business. Have you ever been to the tropics?

Hannah: No, I haven't, and it sounds great. You'll have to fill me in on the details – maybe we can discuss it later when we take a break for lunch.

Jose: Sure, I'd be glad to. So, should we start slugging it out?

Jose is using a joking tone.

Hannah: Ha! I don't think that will be necessary. We've got a lot of common ground here. I'm pretty sure we can work through the rough spots without coming to blows.

Hannah also responds in a joking manner.

Hannah's approach to the negotiation set an effective tone by building rapport with Jose. By beginning the negotiation with a little small talk, Hannah connected with Jose on a personal level before getting down to the serious business of negotiation.

There are natural barriers between any two opposing parties. Each party has different interests and both have the primary goal of ensuring the negotiation meets their respective needs.

Beginning with some small talk – perhaps over coffee, soft drinks, or snacks – can help ease tensions and allow the different sides to get a sense of each other's styles and manners.

Rapport-building techniques aren't used to manipulate the other person. They're ways to establish some sort of connection and increase understanding. Negotiators with a degree of rapport can work together more effectively to develop solutions. In addition to using small talk, there are other techniques for building rapport:

- Be aware of the other person's body language and adjust your own to align. Mirroring body language can be especially important when negotiating with people from cultures other than your own. For example, if your opponent bows as a greeting, you should probably bow in return.

- Try to match the amount of eye contact your opponent makes. If the person is always looking straight at you, it's best to return a similar directness to avoid seeming rude. Bear in mind that cultures differ on this issue. For example, keeping direct eye contact with a work supervisor may be considered aggressive and rude in some cultures.
- Pay attention to verbal style, including tone of voice, pace, and choice of words. If the other negotiator presents information in a quiet tone and calm manner, use a similar style and pace when speaking.
- Be respectful and polite. This means the other party will be more likely to take a cooperative approach. Show that you're interested in the other party's concerns and open to other points of view. Also, when you can honestly do so, you may want to express respect for the other side's skills and experience.

So a state of rapport gives you a better understanding of the other party's point of view while at the same time increases your ability to influence that person. As you build rapport, you make a connection with the other party that will allow you to understand each other beyond the words that are spoken. You'll benefit by having a smoother negotiation session that will allow you to better generate options and increase your chances of reaching an agreement.

FOCUSING ON THE POSITIVE

Focusing on the positive

After a little small talk, the representative of the development firm, Hannah, begins to negotiate with Jose, the head of the planning commission. She employs more techniques to set the tone. Follow along as their negotiation continues.

Jose: I'm not sure how we're going to come to an agreement anytime soon. We have opposing needs. My commission is determined to maintain the historic look of the area, and your mall development is against all the guidelines we've developed.

Hannah: Actually I don't think we're as far apart on the issues as you think. Our firm appreciates the historic character of the town and we're committed to ensuring our architecture and our approach align with the spirit of the town's ordinances. I'm sure that, by working together, we can resolve all the smaller issues.

Jose: But what about the traffic concerns and the impact on the local environment?

Hannah: If we just tackle each individual point together, I'm sure we can find a solution. You've managed to negotiate successful outcomes from several smaller developers in the past. I bet your experience in that regard will be valuable.

Question

Which do you think are effective ways that Hannah focuses on the positive in the dialog with Jose?

Options:

1. She frames the issues as mutual problems to be solved
2. She points to Jose's previous successes
3. She engages in small talk to relieve tensions
4. She ignores Jose's negative comments

Answer

Option 1: This option is correct. Hannah effectively focuses on the positive by framing the issues brought up by Jose as mutual problems to be solved. She is solution focused, rather than problem focused.

Option 2: This is a correct option. Hannah encourages Jose by pointing to his previous successes. Being encouraging is definitely a positive action.

Option 3: This option is incorrect. Hannah addresses some issues brought up by Jose, and doesn't resort to small talk at this point. Engaging in small talk helps to build rapport, which was established in their previous dialog.

Option 4: This is an incorrect option. Hannah doesn't ignore Jose's comments, even though they are negative. Rather, she reframes them in a more positive way.

Hannah sets an effective tone by emphasizing the positive aspects of the negotiation. In addition to focusing on solutions and pointing to Jose's previous successes, she highlights common ground, mutual benefits, and similarities using positive language to express her views. In other words, she emphasizes what can be done, suggests alternatives, and is encouraging. Negative language typically includes words like can't or won't, and often has a subtle tone of blame – which is not the case for Hannah.

In negotiations, the two parties are often tied together somehow. Consider an employee and an employer, a supplier and a buyer, or on the personal level, a parent and a child. It's particularly important to seek a win-win resolution when relationships are ongoing.

Expressing your commitment may seem simple and unnecessary. But you can set a positive tone by sincerely framing your negotiation as a mutual problem you are committed to resolving to the satisfaction of both parties.

Also, throughout the negotiation, watch for opportunities to honestly praise your counterpart's actions. If the other person makes a fair offer or a move in your direction, acknowledge it, even if it doesn't go as far as you'd like.

You can also set a positive tone by selecting a positive environment for both parties to negotiate in. Don't try to put the other person at an uncomfortable disadvantage using the physical surroundings for the negotiation. For example, don't sit behind a big comfortable desk and have the other party pull up a chair. And avoid squaring off across a negotiating table when sitting side by side will convey a more cooperative approach.

BEING CONSISTENT

Being consistent

As Hannah and Jose continue to negotiate aspects of the development project, Hannah employs a different strategy when it comes to the issue of traffic control. Follow along with the negotiation.

Hannah: I'm glad we're working on this together. We've made great progress on the first five points.

Jose: Yes, I'm surprised it's gone this quickly. We've reached some good compromises.

Hannah: Well, unfortunately, that isn't going to happen on the issue of traffic control. It's an absolute requirement that we be allowed to build an access road from each direction.

Hannah speaks with a firm tone.

Jose: Well, we're prepared to allow for two access roads, but four is too many.

Jose is trying to be reasonable.

Hannah: As I said, this is non-negotiable. There's no point in discussing this further unless you agree to four. It's four, or we walk.

Hannah's tone is harsh.
Question
What has gone wrong in Hannah's approach?
Options:
1. She isn't building rapport effectively
2. She isn't being consistent
3. She hasn't done anything wrong

Answer

Hannah isn't being consistent. She has made compromises during the earlier part of their conversation, as indicated by Jose. But now she wants to take a harsher stance, delivering an ultimatum.

Many negotiations fall apart before reaching a solution because the parties fail to build enough trust to negotiate effectively. With a collaborative approach, you should set a consistent tone that suggests you are determined to represent your needs, but also flexible and reasonable enough to work with others.

Inconsistency in a negotiation results in the same problem no matter how it manifests itself. Trust and credibility are lost, for example, if you start out with a reasonable offer and then back up and take a tougher stance. The same is true if you make an outrageous offer at first and then backpeddle, act reasonable, and compromise later on.

Being consistent in your approach and tone will benefit you by building trust and giving you more credibility with the other party.

Hannah's earlier efforts established a collaborative tone for the negotiation. It is inconsistent to then make an extreme or inflexible demand. The other party will be confused. Because Hannah's stance makes her seem untrustworthy, Jose won't know how to act from that point on.

Question

Which actions illustrate how to execute the strategies for setting the right collaborative tone in a negotiation?

Options:

1. Use small talk to reduce tension at the start

2. Point out that most of the issues on the agenda have been resolved, so surely the remaining few will be possible as well

3. Be assertive from the beginning and maintain that approach throughout

4. Be aggressive about the issue you care most about, and reasonable and collaborative about all others

5. Ask about your opponent's personal life to discover information you can take advantage of in the negotiation

Answer

Option 1: This is a correct option. You can build rapport by using small talk at the beginning of a negotiation to put both parties at ease and develop a bond.

Option 2: This is a correct option. Expressing your honest confidence that you'll be able to work together to resolve the issue at hand is a way to focus on positives.

Option 3: This is a correct option. Consistency will build trust and confidence, and set an effective tone throughout the negotiations.

Option 4: This is an incorrect option. Being inconsistent at certain points in your negotiation will erode trust, confuse the other party, and fail to set the right tone.

Option 5: This is an incorrect option. Getting to know your opponent better will help you set the tone by building rapport. But asking personal questions to probe for personal vulnerabilities is more appropriate to a confrontation than a negotiation.

Question

What are the benefits of being able to set the right tone for a negotiation?

Options:

1. You will have greater credibility
2. You will have a smoother negotiation session
3. You will win the most from the negotiation
4. You will reach a conclusion faster

Answer

Option 1: This is a correct option. Setting the right tone means being consistent. When you are consistent, the other party will trust you, and you will have more credibility. Moreover, when you set a positive tone by focusing on mutual gains and solutions, you enhance your credibility as well.

Option 2: This is a correct option. Establishing a collaborative tone gives you a better chance of a smooth negotiation and eventually reaching the agreement stage.

Option 3: This is an incorrect option. Setting a collaborative and positive tone works to make both parties winners to some degree.

Option 4: This is an incorrect option. Setting a positive tone will smooth the process and improve the chances of a mutual win, but it may not make the negotiation faster. For instance, a confrontational approach might skip the small talk and lead to a quick decision to walk away.

SECTION 2 - MAKING A PROPOSAL IN A NEGOTIATION

SECTION 2 - Making a Proposal in a Negotiation

After setting the tone for a negotiation, establishing an agenda, and coming to a basic understanding of how the negotiating process will be executed, the negotiation itself can begin. Although some debate and discussion of the issues may precede making the first proposal, that's when the negotiation truly starts.

Proposals are the cornerstone of the negotiating process, and they must be put forth in the right way to be effective. You must consider whether or not to be the first party to make a proposal and decide how you will present it. To achieve clarity, move things toward a decision, and get maximum results, you should limit the number of issues, structure your message carefully, and use assertive language.

SETTING THE AGENDA AND PROCESS

Setting the agenda and process

After initial greetings and some small talk over coffee, Lloyd, a supplier, and Amara, the buyer, sit down to begin talking about a new contract. Lloyd, the less experienced negotiator, says "Might as well start with what we're proposing for the new terms. We will..." Amara interrupts him, saying "Before we get to negotiating, we need to talk about how we're going to negotiate."

After the opening pleasantries, there are a couple of things to establish before moving on to the negotiation itself: the agenda and the process.

An agenda establishes what will and won't be covered during the negotiations. Both parties benefit from knowing the main issues to be discussed and the peripheral issues that may arise.

To ensure both parties have the same expectations, you should explicitly discuss the process as well. Consider how many meetings you'll have, how long each will be, and whether or not there will be general discussion before the first proposal is made.

Discussing the agenda and process may give you some sense of the other party's frame of mind and style before the actual negotiations begin.

Setting up the agenda and process may also provide opportunities for positioning. For example, you may want to consider who gets to first suggest an agenda and who responds.

Regardless of who goes first, the main objective is to ensure that you and your negotiating partner both understand exactly what will be covered and what won't be.

WHO PROPOSES FIRST?

Who proposes first?

Preparing the agenda and deciding on the process, along with setting the tone, are preliminary actions to the actual negotiation, which begins when one side or the other makes the first proposal.

Proposals are the tentative content of the potential decisions you'll make in the negotiation. They take the meeting beyond debating a problem and move it toward a jointly agreed solution.

As you reach the point of the first proposal, you face a crucial decision: who opens the negotiation? Some say it depends on the situation, but many believe it's always better to let the other party go first. That's because the person who proposes first is the one who first makes their position visible. And the other party gets to see the first proposer's position before making a response.

First proposers reveal valuable information about how they intend to approach the negotiation and what their starting offer is. If you get the other person to go first, you can adjust your initial position in light of what you learn.

You may choose to accept the proposal if it's better than you hoped for, or you may reject it if it's worse than your objectives. But if you go first, you'll never know what the other person might have offered.

Those who say there are situations when you should choose to go first maintain that the decision should be based on whether you're negotiating in unfamiliar or familiar situations.

Unfamiliar situation

It's a good idea to let the other party start when you're on unfamiliar negotiating territory, or if you don't have much information about the other party's position and expectations.

Familiar situation

If you're on familiar ground, have a good idea what a fair settlement would be, and are familiar with the other party, you might choose to go first. Going first could help you convey that you're strong, in charge, and know exactly what you want.

LIMITING THE NUMBER OF ISSUES

Limiting the number of issues

Given the importance of proposals, it's not surprising that negotiators who take care in communicating them do better than those who don't. There are three effective ways to better communicate your proposals:
- Limit the number of issues. This helps ensure your proposal clearly communicates your key needs.
- Structure the message effectively. You can get greater impact from a message by optimizing the order of the presentation. Message structure can help improve clarity.
- Use assertive language. Assertive language helps you communicate your needs clearly and is more suitable to collaborative negotiation than aggressive or submissive speech.

The number of issues that need to be covered in a negotiation varies greatly. The more issues included in each proposal, the less manageable that proposal becomes.

To limit the number of issues, focus each proposal on only a small number of key points. Your arguments will be made stronger if you are succinct and focused.

Try to highlight the points that will be understood and that appeal to the other side's interests.

Repetition of these key points may also increase the degree to which they're understood, and may help to keep everyone focused. But don't repeat too much or you risk losing the interest of the other party.

And if, due to the complexity of the negotiation, it's not possible to keep to fewer than four or five linked issues, your best option may be to deal with each of the issues one at a time.

STRUCTURING THE MESSAGE EFFECTIVELY

Structuring the message effectively

In addition to limiting yourself to just a few issues per proposal, you must structure the proposal message effectively. This begins with making your message clear. When you are clear, you push the other person to greater clarity and decisiveness.

But if your message is complex or ambiguous, or your key points are buried in verbiage, the other person will feel insecure and may – as a matter of caution – respond by being less clear. Accidental miscommunication can do just as much harm as an intentional lie.

Even if the discussion seems to go smoothly, there may be underlying confusion that doesn't get discovered until later. If this happens, you may find yourself back at the negotiating table to resolve the problem or find yourself battling it out in court.

What you say in a proposal and how you say it are both important, but so is when you say it. If you have multiple points to make in a negotiation, the order in which you present them matters. When deciding on the order, remember that anything buried in the middle is more likely to be forgotten according to two basic communication principles – the primacy effect and the recency effect.

Primacy effect

The primacy effect refers to the human tendency to remember the first thing heard in a list. Negotiators can take advantage of this by starting with something the other party wants to hear about, putting the other party in a favorable frame of mind for addressing other issues.

Recency effect

The recency effect is that people tend to remember the last thing heard, especially with long lists and difficult or unfamiliar points. Put complex or multistep procedures at the end of your proposal to take advantage of the recency effect.

Taking into account the primacy and recency effects, you should put your key points or most important requirements at the front and back end of your message to reinforce them.

A little repetition can help the listener take in the information you are presenting. You can achieve this by summarizing and checking understanding periodically.

But use caution when repeating a key point. Beyond a few repetitions, your listener can become saturated and begin to reject the message.

Also, proposals are more effective when they're structured conditionally and when they move from slightly vague to more specific. To accomplish this, use an if/then format for your proposal. For instance, you could vaguely say "If you do this...then I'll consider doing that." This keeps your options open until you learn more about the other side. A little vagueness smoothes negotiations. Getting too specific early on may make you overshoot the other side's needs and cause you to give up more than necessary.

Consider the negotiation involving Lloyd, a representative for a company that supplies raw materials for plastics manufacturing, and Amara, the negotiator for one of the company's customers. Lloyd has opened the discussion by asking Amara what changes to the existing contract her company would like to make.

Amara begins by stating the three main issues that her company needs to address: a reduction in base price, an extension of the contract, and quicker turnaround time. She explains these issues briefly and subtly indicates certain other areas of the contract that her company would consider more negotiable.

In the middle of her presentation, she reiterates the three areas of concern and then wraps up by stating her proposal.

Amara says "If you could consider reducing your base price and delivery turnaround, as well as changing the term of the contract, then we can talk about increasing our volume."

Question

How well do you think Amara structured her proposal and the surrounding discussion?

Options:
1. Amara did very well
2. Amara did not do well

Answer

Amara structured her proposal well. She presented the key points at the beginning and at the end to take advantage of the primacy and recency effects. She also used repetition effectively by mentioning the key points in the middle. In addition, she used the "if/then" format to present the proposal, remaining vague about the exact details at this point in the negotiations.

Amara structured her message effectively by stating her key concerns at the start and end of her proposal. She used an if/then format for the proposal, and was vague because she wanted to test the water before committing herself.

Offers should always be vague, but conditions can be either specific or vague. So it's better for Amara to say "then we can talk about increasing our volume," rather than saying "we can increase our volume by 50%." She could've been more specific with the conditions by saying, for example, "if you increase the term of the contract by 5 years." But her offer should remain vague until she knows more about the nature of the deal and the other party.

As each party makes its proposal, amending it along the way, a little vagueness smoothes the discussion.

USING ASSERTIVE LANGUAGE

Using assertive language

In addition to limiting the issues and structuring the proposal message effectively, choice of words is another critical factor for successful negotiations. Neither aggressive nor submissive language is likely to get you what you want. If bullying the other person or plaintively asking could solve the problem, there probably wouldn't be a negotiation.

To keep the discussion moving forward toward decision making, you should use an assertive approach in the language, form, tone, and content of your proposal.

Avoid proposals like "I hope you can finish by that date" or "Can you at least pay some of our costs?" This kind of hedging leads to poorer deals. This is because the person proposing seems to be seeking the permission of the other party to develop their own proposals.

When you state your proposal assertively, you define the terms of the exchange – what you want in exchange for what you might be prepared to offer.

To be assertive, your conditionally phrased proposals should include statements, not questions. An assertive proposal using an if/then statement would be "If you do this...then I'll do that." The same proposition phrased as a question becomes submissive instead of assertive. "If I do this, will you do that?" Just by changing the proposal to a question, you have changed it from an offer to a request for a favor – a request the other party can easily turn down.

The key is to present your condition first and then your offer. For example, a submissive proposal such as "If we change the requirement for three additional inspectors, would you agree to decreasing turnaround time?" should be stated as "If you decrease turnaround time sufficiently, we might be willing to change the requirement for three additional inspectors."

A few people may be sensitive to direct, assertive language. But by stating what you want, you're not being aggressive – you're being clear. You probably won't get what you want when you ask for things using weak phrasing like "hope for" and "would like."

You should state anything of real importance to you as something you "need" or "require."

You'll sound more confident when you use assertive statements, and they'll move the process along by identifying possible decisions the parties could make.

Question

You are the negotiator for a transportation company negotiating a contract with a manufacturer.

Which are effective ways to communicate your proposal?

Options:

1. Focus on your three most important issues: insurance, price, and safety

2. State the key issues up front, reiterate them once in the middle, and summarize them at the end

3. Tell your negotiating partner that if her company will forego the additional insurance requirement, your company will consider posting a bond

4. Say "If we agree to the two-day delivery requirement, will your firm agree to the computer system upgrade?"

5. Avoid repetition and list your prime objectives at the end of your proposal because of the primacy effect

Answer

Option 1: This is a correct option. You will improve the effectiveness of your proposals if you limit the number of issues. Choosing a handful of the most important issues will make it clear and memorable.

Option 2: This is a correct option. Mentioning your key points at the start and the end is a way to effectively structure your proposal in light of the primacy and recency effects. A reminder in the middle is useful repetition.

Option 3: This is a correct option. Using an if/then statement when communicating a proposal – as opposed to an if/then question – is a way to assertively state your condition and offer.

Option 4: This is an incorrect option. If your if/then proposition is framed as a question, it's submissive. Changing it to a statement will make for a more assertive and effective proposal.

Option 5: This is an incorrect option. The primacy effect would have you list prime objectives on the front end of your proposal. The recency effect applies to the back end. Also, a little repetition can be a good thing.

SECTION 3 - RESPONDING TO THE OTHER PARTY IN A NEGOTIATION

SECTION 3 - Responding to the Other Party in a Negotiation

As the first proposal is made and the negotiation begins, everything changes. Responding to the other person's comments, information, and proposals is a crucial skill in reaching a solution.

To ensure your responses stay positive and the dialogue continues to move forward, apply three broad techniques: avoid a quick response, check your understanding, and clear the air.

AVOIDING A QUICK RESPONSE

Avoiding a quick response

If framing and presenting your proposal were all there was to negotiation, most negotiations would end quickly – in failure. But negotiation is about reaching agreement. This requires not only good communication of a proposal but also flexibility, movement on the issues, and the ability to respond appropriately to the other side's proposals.

The adage "no battle plan survives the first contact with the opposition" applies to negotiations as well. With the first proposal, the situation changes and becomes more fluid. From that point on, your ability to respond and adjust becomes crucial. Three techniques can help you respond positively throughout a negotiation: avoid a quick response, check your understanding, and clear the air.

Quick responses

Your first impulse might be to say "No way! You must be joking." or "Dream on!" But these kinds of knee-jerk negative responses won't keep things moving forward in a positive fashion.

Developing a few simple habits can help you avoid an overly quick reaction that might slow down or put your negotiation at risk. To avoid responding too quickly, don't interrupt with your first reaction, take time to acknowledge the other side's points, and phrase your response positively.

Don't interrupt with your first reaction

A quick response means you don't take time to think things through and consider the merits of what the other person has said – and this person will know it. Don't interrupt or immediately reject the other person's statement with responses like "You must be joking" or "No way."

Acknowledge the other side's points

Take the time to acknowledge the other side's points before responding. An overly quick counterproposal effectively acts as rejection of what was just said to you. Indicating your appreciation and comprehension gives your counterarguments more weight because the other party will feel it has been heard.

Phrase your response positively

Try to avoid words that escalate problem situations. The word "you" personalizes an action and sounds accusatory. The word "but" negates the other person's reasoning. And absolutes such as "can't", "won't", and "never" slow down or even stop progress.

Improve your responses by paying attention to sentence structure. For example, always explain why you disagree before you indicate your disagreement. If you start with "I don't agree..." that's all the other person will hear. The other person immediately starts thinking about persuading you otherwise, instead of listening to your explanation.

For example, you could say something like "The figures indicate an increase, not a decrease. So I don't agree."

Consider the contract negotiation between Lloyd, who represents a chemical supply company, and the negotiator for his biggest customer, Amara. Immediately after Amara states her proposal, Lloyd responds with one of his own. Follow along to learn how Amara reacts.

Lloyd: If you give us a 15% increase in volume each year for the three-year life of the contract, we'll offer to lower the base price by 3%.

Amara: That doesn't align with what I just proposed. You didn't mention turnaround time. That's a major concern for us. And I was talking about a five-year contract.

Lloyd: Oh, right. A five-year contract would be good, but we need a 45% increase in volume overall.

Amara: There's no way that's going to happen. A volume increase of 45% is outrageous!

Lloyd: I disagree. That's just a 9% increase per year, and if we're doing a good job, that would be to your benefit.

Question

Who do you think failed to apply good techniques for responding in the negotiation between Lloyd and Amara?

Options:

1. Lloyd
2. Amara
3. Both

Answer

Both Lloyd and Amara made poor responses. Amara reacted with a quick and adamant rejection of Lloyd's

45% increase. In turn, Lloyd expressed his disagreement first and his reasoning second.

CHECKING YOUR UNDERSTANDING

Checking your understanding

As the other side presents its proposals, data, and overall case, you need to thoroughly evaluate what's being said. Make sure what's said is factual, includes all relevant data, and the information is being represented accurately. And before you respond, check your understanding.

To ensure you understand the other person, simply listen. Don't think ahead to the next point you want to make. Keep your head in the game and pay attention to what's being said so you don't miss key information and respond incorrectly. If it becomes obvious that you weren't listening, you'll lose credibility.

Often, the side that does best in a negotiation is the side that asks the most questions.

Ask questions for clarification

Check your understanding by asking questions for clarification. Doing so regularly helps you keep things on track and gets you more information from the other party – which translates to more negotiating power.

Use questions to fill gaps in your knowledge

Using questions helps you fill gaps in your knowledge while at the same time reduces the amount of information you divulge. If the other side is answering questions, the person will be too busy providing information to get any out of you.

Probe for information in a neutral or positive way

Probe for information in a neutral or positive way, saying things like "What exactly did you mean when you mentioned updating the equipment?" or "Could you clarify what would be included in 'incidental expenses'?"

Avoid too many yes-or-no questions

Avoid questions that can be answered with a simple yes or no. These closed-ended questions don't get you much information, and too many of them can make a conversation sound more like an interrogation.

Questions are the best way to address the other side's faulty logic. Rather than saying "You're not making any sense," use questions to bring faults to light and allow the other person to discover the error. Clarification questions can also be used to challenge people's perceptions. People frequently generalize about things, and by questioning, you can get the other person to be more specific and target the actual problem.

Of course, bad questioning techniques can negate any positive effects of asking questions. For example, you shouldn't ask a question and immediately answer it yourself.

You should also avoid making a lengthy statement followed by a closed-ended question like "Isn't that true?" This approach doesn't help you learn much, as you're the one providing all the information before trying to trap the person into agreeing with you.

Also avoid leading questions and judgmental questions such as "Didn't you just say ...?" or "Why have you ignored...?"

Summarizing also tests your understanding. You can clarify agreements and make sure everyone's perceptions align by saying something like "Before we move on to other things, let's make sure we're all clear on what's been agreed on so far."

By establishing what's already been agreed upon, a summary helps everyone recognize the progress that's being made. Summarizing can also be used to slow down the negotiation process while you gather your thoughts.

As Lloyd and Amara continue their contract negotiation, Amara is careful to check her understanding. Follow along to learn how Amara uses questions effectively.

Lloyd: So we've agreed my company will lower your base price by 3% and change the term of the contract to 5 years in return for a 30% increase in volume and a 1% share of annual earnings.

Amara: What exactly do you consider "annual earnings?" Does that refer to income, profits, or profits after taxes?

Lloyd: Profits after taxes would make the most sense.

Amara: You're aware that, as a startup company, it may be several years before we show an after-tax profit, right?

Lloyd: Good point. Thanks for clarifying that.

Lloyd started by summarizing to clarify his understanding. And Amara effectively used questions first to get more detail about what would be defined as "annual earnings" and then to ensure Lloyd's understanding matched her own.

CLEARING THE AIR

Clearing the air

Emotions can affect communication in any situation. Often, negotiations are made more challenging because two complete strangers must communicate while being affected by emotions. To negotiate without misunderstanding, be aware of the emotions involved - both your own and the other party's – and find a way of clearing the air.

When emotions get in the way, the best solution is to make them explicit. This may be all that's needed to ease a situation where parties are getting angry, nervous, or excited.

Many people think skilled negotiators must keep their feelings to themselves and negotiate in a detached and logical way. But sometimes it's more effective to own up to what you're feeling.

For example, you might say "I'm starting to feel uncomfortable with the personal nature of some of these questions. Could you tell me how they apply to the job we're discussing?"

Reacting to an emotional outburst

The key to dealing with an emotional outburst or attack is to avoid responding with an emotional outburst of your own. Maintain self-control and redirect the energy as constructively as possible. Try to keep things focused on what you're trying to achieve.

To avoid escalating an emotional situation, allow the other party to calm down. Then tell the other person you can relate to the feelings and concerns expressed.

You may want to paraphrase what the other person said to ensure you understand both the problem and what that person wants you to do about it.

It can be a good idea to break the rhythm of the negotiation after dealing with an emotional outburst. You could take a short refreshment break or step outside for some fresh air. A little time for reflection can diffuse the tension.

When an issue makes another negotiator tense, you should acknowledge it, taking care to put it in terms of how it affects you, rather than what you think the other person feels. For example, a statement such as "You're angry with me because I'm less experienced" should be expressed as "I feel like I'm a source of frustration because of my lack of experience."

As Lloyd and Amara negotiate, they reach an impasse on the issue of subcontracting some of the chemical production. Follow along to learn how emotion enters into their negotiation.

Lloyd: To meet your need for a lower base price, we need to subcontract the production of several chemicals. There's no way for us to make a profit without outsourcing some production.

Amara: Our company is keen on keeping all parts of our supply chain locally owned. I don't think I can budge on this issue.

Lloyd: I know for a fact that some of your other contracts allow subcontracting and outsourcing.

Amara: Not ones I had anything to do with!

Lloyd: I understand your company tries to help the local economy and I appreciate that. But I can see this issue is a source of personal frustration for you as well. Am I right?

Amara: It is. My brother just lost his job to a competitor overseas and he's having a tough time.

Lloyd: Thanks for bringing that out in the open. I can understand how that affects you. Why don't we take a short break and get some fresh air?

Question

Which negotiator applied appropriate techniques for clearing the air and making emotions explicit in Amara and Lloyd's negotiation?

Options:

1. Lloyd
2. Amara

Answer

Lloyd remained calm in the face of an outburst and acknowledged an issue that made Amara tense. And he suggested a brief break to allow tensions to ease.

CHAPTER 4 - PERSUADING

CHAPTER 4 - Persuading
SECTION 1 - <u>Strategies for Being a Persuasive Negotiator</u>
SECTION 2 - <u>Dealing with a Difficult Person in a Negotiation</u>

SECTION 1 - STRATEGIES FOR BEING A PERSUASIVE NEGOTIATOR

SECTION 1 - Strategies for Being a Persuasive Negotiator

Good negotiators are persuasive. To persuade others, you need to put yourself in their position, build trust, and establish a dialog with them. Putting yourself in the other person's position means finding out about that person's interests and needs. Empowering questions can help you do this.

You can build trust by being confident, sincere, and honest. It also helps to establish credibility and use only verifiable facts and statistics during the negotiation. Establishing a dialog with the other party entails gradually revealing your position and listening to the other party's responses. It's also important to use breaks strategically.

THREE STRATEGIES FOR PERSUASION

Three strategies for persuasion

Marianne is stressed by her daily commute to work. By the time she gets to the office, she's spent an hour in heavy traffic. And she faces the same drive in the other direction after work. Marianne decides to talk to her boss, Douglas, about her problem to find out if they can negotiate a solution.

Douglas: Hi, Marianne. What's on your mind?

Marianne: It's my commute. It's killing me, Douglas. I'm exhausted by the time I get here, and I spend much the day dreading the drive home. I've noticed some of my coworkers work from home a couple of days a week. I'd like to do that too. I'd be less stressed, and I'd be more productive.

Douglas: Well, Marianne, we do offer that option to our high-achieving workers. Do you think you're in that category?

Marianne: Well, maybe not yet. But when I'm working from home, I can be much more effective. What do you think?

Douglas: Hmmm. I'm not so sure. Have you considered flextime? You could arrange your working hours to avoid the worst of the traffic.

Marianne: I can't do flextime. It's impossible. The best option for me is to work from home.

Douglas: Well, maybe you should consider going part time. Then you'd only have to come to work two or three days a week.

Marianne: But I need a full-time job. You're not listening to me.

Douglas: Marianne, working from home is a privilege you haven't earned. If you can't do flextime or go part time, I'm afraid I don't have anything else to offer.

Marianne: That's not fair. I hoped you'd be more flexible than this. I guess I'm going to have to look for another job.

Marianne didn't get very far, did she?

She listed her demands up front in a rush. She was impatient and didn't listen to Douglas. She made demands, and she refused to compromise on her position.

Obviously, these tactics won't work to persuade someone to agree with your position.

Marianne would have gotten a lot further had she used a little persuasion. Remember, to be successful in negotiating, you shouldn't demand or threaten. Instead, use persuasion to convince the other party why you should have your needs met.

Question

Persuasive people use specific techniques to help them achieve their goals.

Which techniques do you think are important in persuasion?

Options:
1. Encourage a dialog
2. Ask questions
3. Listen actively
4. Make concessions
5. Use long monologues to communicate
6. Withhold information

Answer

Persuasive people encourage dialog with the other party, ask questions instead of making statements, listen actively, and make concessions to the other party's changing expectations.

A persuasive person is one who:
- establishes a dialog with the other party,
- asks questions to learn about the other party's needs and wants,
- listens actively to gain information and establish rapport, and
- makes concessions in time with the other party's changing expectations.

Using persuasion, a negotiation becomes a collaboration. The result? Both parties win and get something they want.

Persuasive negotiators use three important strategies. They put themselves in the other party's position, they build trust, and they establish a dialog with the other person. With these strategies, persuaders gain the insights and knowledge required to convince the other party of their position.

Put yourself in the other party's position

You can't sell something unless you know what the other person is willing to buy. To find this out, you put yourself in the other party's position and try to learn the other person's values, desires, and motivations.

Build trust

To encourage others to be open and give you what you want, you have to earn their trust. People won't want to deal with someone they don't trust.

Establish a dialog

Another word for negotiation is conversation. It's important to engage the other person in a dialog. Ask questions to learn more about who the other person is and what terms are acceptable to them. You must also be prepared to make concessions and suggest alternatives in order to move forward.

PUT YOURSELF IN THE OTHER'S POSITION

Put yourself in the other's position

The first strategy in persuasive negotiation is to put yourself in the other party's position. Remember, in any transaction, people are primarily interested in how they will benefit.

The other party in the negotiation will be most open to persuasion when you show concern for their interests and needs. To persuade others to give you what you need, you must learn what they need.

Then you can explain – or frame – your position in terms of how it benefits the other person. Try not to focus on how it benefits you or your position. You'll lose the other party's interest.

Consider how Chris, a project manager, uses framing to get additional funds for his project budget. Chris is developing a web site for his company. During development, Chris learns about new features he hadn't planned for but wants to include.

This would mean requesting a 30% increase in his project's budget.

Chris's manager, Marie, is concerned with cost control. Chris knows she won't want to give him more money.

To figure out how to "sell" his position, Chris puts himself in Marie's position.

Chris knows that, as a manager, Marie is concerned with improving performance and keeping costs down. So he frames his request in terms of how the proposed new features of his web site will improve system and organizational performance and save money.

By emphasizing improved performance and downplaying the additional costs, Chris obtains a 25% increase in his budget from Marie. Both Chris and Marie are satisfied with their negotiation.

Effective framing is dependent on finding out what the other party wants. One way to do this is to ask questions and listen to the answers. Skillful questioning can reveal important information about the other party's values, beliefs, and intentions. It also helps you build rapport with the other party – it shows you're interested in creating a collaborative environment.

Not all questions are created equal though. You should ask questions that are open-ended and designed to move the negotiations forward.

These kinds of questions are called empowering questions.

Disempowering questions, on the other hand, don't move the discussion forward. This may be because they're close-ended or overly negative. For example, they may focus on a problem, rather than a solution. They may even cause the negotiations to stall.

Question

Imagine you're negotiating a starting salary and benefits with your new employer, but the offer is lower than you'd expected.

Which questions do you think are empowering?

Options:

1. "I don't understand your reasoning; could you explain it to me please?"
2. "We seem to be stuck. What would it take for us to move forward with this negotiation?"
3. "Is there anything I can do to get you to increase the amount of insurance coverage you're offering?"
4. "We seem to be stuck. Why aren't we making any progress?"
5. "Don't you think I'm worth the salary I'm asking for?"

Answer

Option 1: This option is correct. The question is empowering because it's open-ended and puts the focus on the other person.

Option 2: This option is correct. It's an empowering question because it's open-ended and because it focuses on solutions to a stalemate.

Option 3: This option is correct. This question is empowering. It's open-ended and helps the negotiator find out what's necessary to get the increase.

Option 4: This option is not correct. This is a disempowering question because it focuses on the problem. Asking this question would produce a list of reasons why you're not making progress, but none of these reasons would be solutions to your stalemate.

Option 5: This option is not correct. This is a disempowering question; it requires a yes/no answer. When the other party answers it, the negotiations could be at an end.

In addition to using framing and asking empowering questions, another important technique for putting yourself in the other party's position is to encourage the other party to change positions without losing face.

It's rare for a negotiation to result in the other party agreeing to everything you ask for. But it's your responsibility to help the other party understand the benefits of your proposal and give them time to change their views.

One way to do this is to make concessions or offer alternatives that are of no risk to you but offer some benefit to the other party. People will often agree to a concession or alternative when they're stuck on a negotiating point. It allows them to save face and "win" the negotiation.

Hypothetical questions can be very helpful when you're floating alternative proposals for the other party to consider. Imagine you're selecting members for a project team. You want to include Yushiko on your team, but a coworker will only agree to including Jason. You could break the stalemate by proposing an alternative, couched in a hypothetical question. You might say, "Well, if you're not interested in Yushiko, what would you say to including Philip? His qualifications are similar to both Yushiko's and Jason's."

Remember Marianne? She still wants to find a solution to her commuting problem. Marianne knows her first negotiation with Douglas was a disaster. She's done some research about putting herself in the other party's position, and she's ready to discuss the issue with Douglas again.

Follow along to learn how Marianne handles her negotiation this time.

Douglas: Hi, Marianne. What's going on?

Marianne: Hi, Douglas. I've been thinking some more about my commuting problem. I understand that I'm unable to work from home, but I'm hoping there's another solution.

Douglas: OK. What are your thoughts?

Marianne: Well, flextime is problematic, but I've been wondering about part-time e work. Can you explain what's involved?

Douglas: Sure. People who work part time are required to be in the office 20 hours a week. You'd keep your benefits, but you'd be an hourly employee, not salaried as you are now. I have to tell you though, I don't think that you going part time would work for us.

Marianne: Oh? Could you explain a little further?

Douglas: At the moment, it wouldn't be a problem. But during the winter, when production is heavy, I need full-time people.

Marianne: Hmmm. What would you say to a situation where I'd work a minimum of 20 hours per week, but beyond that, I'd work as many hours as you'd need me? During the summer, I'd be part time, but during the winter, I could work a full week.

Douglas: You know, that could actually work out very well for me. I could use you to level out the peaks and valleys of my production cycle. Let me have a few days to think this through. Give me a call on Thursday, and we'll brainstorm some of the issues.

Question

Marianne did a lot better in this negotiation than she did her first time around.

Which strategies for putting herself in Douglas's position did Marianne use effectively?

Options:

1. She framed her request so Douglas could perceive it as a benefit to him
2. She used questions rather than statements to find out what Douglas needed
3. She encouraged Douglas to change his mind about her going part time by emphasizing benefits to him
4. She focused on how working only 20 hours a week would help her so that Douglas would understand her position too
5. She framed her request in a way that would allow her to keep her employment benefits

Answer

Option 1: This option is correct. Marianne offered to work more or fewer hours to help Douglas staff for production peaks and valleys.

Option 2: This option is correct. Marianne didn't present her position with statements. Instead, she used questions to find out what Douglas's ideas were.

Option 3: This option is correct. At first, Douglas didn't think having Marianne go part time would be possible. Marianne conceded a fixed schedule to help him understand that her part-time status could actually benefit him.

Option 4: This option is not correct. Marianne used questions to find out what Douglas needed. Then she framed her request with his needs in mind. Focusing on how part-time work will help her is not an effective way of understanding the other party's side.

Option 5: This option is not correct. She framed her request in terms of helping Douglas meet his staffing needs, not as a way to keep her benefits.

BUILD TRUST

Build trust

You can't persuade someone to accept your proposition if that person doesn't trust you. Building trust is the second important persuasive negotiation strategy. It's linked with putting yourself in the other party's position because when you understand the other party's history, culture, and perspective, you send the message that you're committed to the negotiation and the relationship – a key step in trust building.

To build trust, you must be sincere and honest. This may mean explaining your limitations, as well as your strengths.

And it helps to explain your demands fully and honestly so the other party understands your position. For example, if you state that you charge more commission for international sales but don't explain why, the other party may doubt your motivations. Are you trying to make more money at their expense?

To inspire trust in others, you must also show confidence in yourself and in the benefits and advantages of your negotiating position. People are drawn to confident individuals. If you show fear or doubt, the party you're negotiating with may perceive it as a lack of confidence in your product or service. Trust will not be given if you don't appear confident.

Consider Jack and Nadia. They work together in the Human Resources Department, and they have roughly equivalent knowledge and time in their positions. However, the coworkers are very different.

Jack

Jack is honest and open with other people. He's learned how to accept criticism and feedback with grace, and he's not afraid to admit when he's wrong. Jack learns from his mistakes and from the input and advice of others. He expects the best from others, and he usually gets it.

Nadia

Nadia is closed off and mistrustful of other people. She reacts defensively to criticism and doesn't accept advice from others. Nadia can't recognize her limitations, so she tends to oversell her abilities. Her unrealistic self-image results in unrealistic goal-setting. Nadia expects the worst, and generally gets it.

Who would you trust more?

Jack is more likely to inspire trust. He's confident in himself, which draws other people to him. This enables Jack to build trust.

You might not trust Nadia. Her lack of confidence and inability to be open with others tend to make people suspicious of her motives.

A sense of confidence is foundational for an even more important attribute – credibility. Credibility is key to your ability to persuade others.

People often don't trust what they see and hear. To be an effective persuader, you have to overcome this natural skepticism.

Begin by making a good first impression. You must look and act polished and professional. When you interact with people, make eye contact and show an interest in what they say. And don't be negative about others, especially your competition.

Then present your qualifications and experience. If other parties in the negotiation don't know you, ask someone they do know to vouch for you. This enables you to "borrow" their credibility until you establish your own. It also allows you to avoid the appearance of bragging when it's this third party who presents your qualifications.

During the negotiation, be careful to use only verifiable facts, figures, and statistics to reinforce your points. Use credible references, and always cite your sources. Credible information from outside sources makes a greater impact than only your own opinions.

Question

You're meeting with Phyllis to negotiate a new hourly rate for your consulting business. You've never worked with Phyllis before.

Which actions are appropriate for building Phyllis's trust?

Options:

1. Be direct and truthful when you explain why you need a higher hourly rate

2. Emphasize what is important about your service in an assured manner

3. Give Phyllis some information that makes your competition look bad

4. Using charts and statistics, show Phyllis how your service has increased her company's profits and productivity

5. Hide your true motives from Phyllis until you're ready to confront her with your position

6. Dress for success

Answer

Option 1: This option is correct. You can show Phyllis you're trustworthy by being open, sincere, and honest.

Option 2: This option is correct. Confidence is compelling and inspires trust.

Option 3: This option is not correct. Making negative remarks about your competition will reflect badly on you. It won't inspire trust.

Option 4: This option is correct. If you use facts, figures, and statistics, make sure they're correct and that Phyllis can verify them.

Option 5: This option is not correct. Honesty is the best policy. It's one thing to strategize how to present your position, but it's quite another to hide it and then spring it on the other party. You risk alienating Phyllis this way.

Option 6: This option is correct. You only have one chance to make a good first impression, so look polished and professional.

ESTABLISH A DIALOG

Establish a dialog

So far, you've examined two persuasion strategies: putting yourself in the other party's position and building trust. A third strategy – establishing a dialog with the other party – focuses on how you communicate.

You can't negotiate successfully by laying out your position in a monologue. Beginners often make this mistake. Remember, negotiation is conversation.

The problem with a monologue approach is that you give your arguments away too early. It also doesn't leave room for give and take. In other words, you aren't able to change the way you present your case in light of the other person's arguments.

A much better strategy is to develop a dialog with the other parties. Reveal your position gradually, giving others the opportunity to comment on your position, and listen carefully as they reveal their own views. The advantage of doing this is that you can modify your position as you learn about the other party's views.

During your conversation, be sure to listen attentively to what the other party has to say. Active listening can provide insights about the other person's thinking process and point of view that will be useful to you in the negotiating process.

Pay attention to both the verbal and body language of the other party. You must learn how to ignore distractions, not interrupt, and show concern for the speaker. It's very important not to argue or judge what's being said.

When you listen attentively, you often deepen the sense of rapport that you have with the other party, which can result in a more trusting relationship.

It's also crucial to create a problem-solving atmosphere for your discussion. You want to focus on finding a solution that both you and the other party can be happy with. To do this, use empowering questions that focus on solutions, not barriers. And avoid "you" language that would turn a negotiation into a win-lose battle.

From time to time, a negotiation can become heated. Or you may need some extra time to consider new points or proposals. When this happens, don't be afraid to suggest taking a break.

Good negotiators make effective use of adjournments.

Simply say, "That's an interesting idea, but I need a little time to consider it. Let's take a break and resume in half an hour." Or, "We seem to be getting bogged down. I think it might be a good idea if we take a quick break at this point – how about ten minutes?"

Question

You're negotiating with Timothy to change a series of milestone dates on an important project. Timothy doesn't want to change the dates, but you do.

Which actions can you take to establish a dialog with him?

Options:

1. Explain one of your reasons for wanting to change the dates and listen to Timothy's response 2. Listen carefully to what Timothy has to say about resetting the dates

3. When Timothy's objections frustrate you, suggest a ten-minute break

4. Focus on the problems that resetting the dates may present

5. Lay out your position at the beginning of the negotiation so Timothy is clear where you stand

Answer

Option 1: This option is correct. It's best to reveal your position gradually to get feedback from the other side and develop a dialog with that person.

Option 2: This option is correct. Listening can provide information about Timothy's goals and what he needs. It can provide insights about the other person's thinking process and point of view that will be useful to you in the negotiating process.

Option 3: This option is correct. Taking a break can help you cool off, and it allows an opportunity to reset the atmosphere of a negotiation.

Option 4: This option is not correct. You need to take a solutions-focused approach. Focusing on the problems could cause Timothy to become entrenched in his position.

Option 5: This option is not correct. It's better to reveal your position gradually so that you can adjust it as Timothy's needs become more clear.

SECTION 2 - DEALING WITH A DIFFICULT PERSON IN A NEGOTIATION

SECTION 2 - Dealing with a Difficult Person in a Negotiation

Sometimes, you'll have to negotiate with people who don't want to cooperate with you. For instance, an aggressive negotiator wants to treat every discussion as a win-lose battle. A bully wants to achieve goals by intimidation. An avoider doesn't want to commit if it leads to confrontation.

You need some tools for dealing with difficult people, so you can achieve your goals.

First, remain calm and control your emotions. If you lose your cool, you could be playing right into the other party's hands. Second, use assertive, gentle confrontation to point out the other party's difficult behavior and gain the person's agreement to change. Third, seek alternatives to a position that seems to be a sticking point. And last, use breaks judiciously. A break gives people time to cool off and think.

DEALING WITH DIFFICULT PEOPLE

Dealing with difficult people

The negotiating process can be hard, and it's even harder when you have to negotiate with difficult people. Would you know what to do with a bully who's intent on dominating you? Or with a person who actively avoids having a productive dialog? What about a person whose emotions are out of control? If you don't know how to handle these kinds of people, you could be in for a frustrating and ineffective negotiating session.

What you need are some good techniques in your negotiation toolkit, which will benefit you when you need to deal with difficult people.

These techniques will increase your chances of reaching an agreement.

And they can keep you from getting thrown off balance when you encounter people who try to intimidate or avoid you.

IDENTIFYING A DIFFICULT PERSON

Identifying a difficult person

So, what constitutes a difficult person? To answer that question, consider three coworkers: Sue, Harlan, and Elliott. All three are considered difficult.

Sue

Sue, like many people, thinks of a negotiation as a competitive activity. She wants to win. If this means that you must lose, so much the better.

Harlan

Harlan is a bully. He wants to intimidate you and scare you into accepting his position.

Elliott

Elliott is a people pleaser and an avoider. He hates conflict and will avoid it at all costs. In a negotiation, he may say things he doesn't mean, or not tell you what he wants, just to avoid upsetting you.

Sue, Harlan, and Elliott are three distinct types of difficult people – the competitive negotiator, the bully, and the avoider. However, many people have varying degrees of these characteristics.

Dealing with difficult people and difficult behavior requires using a combination of techniques, including controlling your emotions, using assertive but gentle confrontation, seeking alternatives, and using breaks strategically.

CONTROLLING YOUR EMOTIONS

Controlling your emotions

Many negotiations generate powerful emotions, which are often expressed as anger or aggression. Anger and aggression are also negotiating "strategies" that can be used to throw you off track. If the other party becomes angry or loses control, it's very important that you remain in control of your emotions.

When you control your emotions, you're aware of and in control of your voice, body, and facial expressions. If the other party catches you even rolling your eyes, you could be in for a difficult time. Don't lose your cool, don't overreact, and don't let the person's behavior push you off your game. Stay focused on your goal.

Consider this situation. You've just presented an alternative suggestion in a negotiation with Joaquin, who suddenly becomes very angry. He pounds the table, jabs his finger at you, and begins to shout. This reaction takes you by complete surprise, and you lose your temper. At this point, Joaquin has you where he wants you. He's used anger as a strategy to make you lose focus, and he's gained the upper hand. You'd have been better off if you'd remained calm during Joaquin's outburst.

Question

You're meeting with Lin, a coworker, to negotiate dividing up some work responsibilities. Lin has more seniority than you do, and she's used to getting her own way. Before you begin your discussion, Lin aggressively states, "I've already decided which responsibilities I want, and I've made a list of the responsibilities I'd like you to take on."

Which action is appropriate for you to take?

Options:

1. Say in a strong voice, "Back off! I don't work for you."
2. Tell Lin in a soft voice, "I'm not sure about this."
3. State, "OK. I guess that's fine."
4. Keep your cool and say calmly, "Before we make any decisions, Lin, we need to talk about this."

Answer

Option 1: This option is not correct. Responding with anger isn't likely to faze Lin at all. You could easily escalate the situation into an angry confrontation.

Option 2: This option is not correct. Lin wants to intimidate you into submission. A weak response like this isn't likely to work with her.

Option 3: This option is not correct. You don't want to give in until you've had a chance to find out what Lin has "assigned" to you.

Option 4: This is the correct option. Remaining calm and asserting yourself is the right way to respond. Don't overreact, and don't let Lin intimidate you into abandoning your goals.

USING ASSERTIVE BUT GENTLE CONFRONTATION

Using assertive but gentle confrontation

Staying calm is the first thing you have to do, but it's equally important to address the other person's difficult behavior. If you let the other party get away with bad behavior, it will only continue. The best way to address difficult behavior is to use assertive but gentle confrontation. Calmly point out to the other party in a nonjudgmental way the negative effects the behavior is having on your discussions.

Consider, for example, that you need to negotiate with a small subcontractor whose staff doesn't return e-mails or phone calls, sometimes for days. The subcontractor provides unique services, so you can't just replace it with a more responsive vendor. Instead, you could try gentle confrontation. You could say, "We really love your company's services, but there's a problem we need to resolve. Your staff's lack of response to our communications has become a real problem for our team."

When you confront the other party, it's important that you focus on the behavior and not the person. Don't use "you" language or sound judgmental. If you insult the other person, you could cause them to lose face or dignity, and this could result in verbal warfare.

Also, be straightforward. Be honest, but don't lecture the person, as this could result in defensiveness or provoke a strong reaction.

And listen carefully without interruption. Allowing the person to explain the behavior or rationalize is important to saving face.

Once you've pointed out the difficult behavior, tell the other party how you expect the behavior to change. Be specific, and ask for the other party's agreement to change.

For example, you might say, "From here on out, I expect an improvement in our communications. Could you agree to return phone calls and e-mails the same day we send them?"

Look the other person in the eye when you ask for agreement, and look for acknowledgment of your request. Agreement signifies the other person takes responsibility for the behavior and for changing it.

Question

You're negotiating with James to buy a large shipment of dress shirts. In the past, James has raised and lowered his prices arbitrarily. He seems on the verge of doing this again.

How should you respond to James's behavior?

Options:

1. Confront James and tell him that indecisiveness is not a career-enhancing characteristic

2. Describe the specific effects that James's price changes have on your business

3. Tell James that if he can't commit to keeping his prices level, you'll have to take your business elsewhere

4. Ask James if he could commit to keeping the prices level or raising them only slightly over the contract year

Answer

Option 1: This option is not correct. You need to focus on the behavior, not the person. Approaching James about indecisiveness is almost guaranteed to anger him.

Option 2: This option is correct. Gently confront James about the behavior that is problematic for you.

Option 3: This option is not correct. This may be true, but this kind of aggressive ultimatum could well result in James's telling you, "Go ahead." You should try a gentle but assertive approach, not an aggressive one.

Option 4: This option is correct. After you've described the effects of the arbitrary price changes on your business, you should ask James to keep the prices level or agree to only a slight increase.

SEEKING ALTERNATIVES

Seeking alternatives

From time to time in a negotiation, you'll arrive at an impasse. For instance, you may be negotiating with a person who wants something that you're unable or unwilling to give, or vice versa. When this happens, you may be able to work around the impasse by seeking alternatives.

For example, you're negotiating with a customer in a sale of auto parts when the customer demands an extended warranty as a condition of the sale. This practice isn't allowed in your industry, so you can't agree to it.

However, if you refuse outright, the negotiation may stall, or the customer may walk away.

To prevent this from happening, you could offer an alternative. Instead of the extended warranty, you could offer to deliver parts days faster than the competition guarantees. While this may not be what the other party ultimately wants, the alternative is valuable and is better than nothing.

Another way to deal with the situation is ask the other party for alternatives. You might say, "I'm afraid I can't offer an extended warranty. What else could I offer that you'd agree to?" Asking the other party to suggest an alternative shows you want to continue the negotiation, just on different terms.

Offering alternatives can work out well for you; it can enhance your credibility and show that you're willing to be reasonable.

Skilled negotiators know the alternatives they're willing to offer – and settle for – before the negotiation even starts. It's wise to know in advance what you're willing to settle for and think it through.

However, it's also important not to get locked into these alternatives.

New alternatives often come to light during negotiations as you gain new information and perspectives on your position, as well as that of the other party.

TAKING A BREAK

Taking a break

Another way to deal with difficult people in a negotiation is by simply taking a break. When tempers flare, when people become fixed on an idea and won't budge, or when difficult behavior reaches a peak, it may be time to step away from the negotiating table for awhile. A break allows people time to cool off and think. A strategically timed break can improve the atmosphere considerably.

Skilled negotiators use three different break techniques when working with difficult people:
- they simply ask to take a break,
- they create a distraction to temporarily refocus people, and
- they break to focus attention on the behavior they want stopped.

Ask to take a break

It can be useful to pause the action when people become intent on their positions and refuse to budge. Leaving the negotiations for a moment to get coffee or a snack can refresh people and give everyone time to think. It's often possible to resolve a stalemate or change the subject when you return from a break.

Create a distraction

Creating a distraction by telling a joke or a funny story can stop the momentum of someone's difficult behavior. Be careful, though. If your timing is wrong, this approach can reduce your credibility and weaken your negotiating position.

Focus attention on behavior

Sometimes, you must name the difficult behavior and state what you want it replaced with. For example, after listening to a group of peers talk about weekend plans for 10 minutes, you might say, "Let's get back to discussing the project budget. If we can't agree on this budget by the end of the day, we'll miss our project start date."

Question

Imagine that you're negotiating with Rania about dividing a project between the two of you. Rania tends to be very aggressive, and she wants to dominate the discussion.

Through gentle confrontation, you've gotten Rania to agree not to fly off the handle whenever you suggest alternatives. But suddenly, Rania loses her temper and begins pounding the desk.

How would you deal with this situation?

Options:

1. Walk out of the room and reschedule the negotiation for another time

2. Tell a joke or a personal story to deflect Rania's aggression

3. Gently confront Rania about how her behavior is preventing the two of you from reaching a solution

4. Remain in control of your own emotions

5. Ask Rania's supervisor to deal with Rania's difficult behavior

Answer

Option 1: This option is not correct. There may be times when walking out of a meeting is appropriate, but there are many strategies you should try before you do this.

Option 2: This option is correct. Telling a joke or interjecting a personal story is a way of breaking the tension of a negotiation. It can help reset the atmosphere to one of mutual problem solving.

Option 3: This option is correct. Be straightforward and nonjudgmental, and tell Rania how her aggressive behavior hinders the negotiation. Then try to gain her agreement to modify her difficult behavior.

Option 4: This option is correct. To be effective, you must remain in control of your own emotions. Losing control could give a "victory" to the other party in the negotiation.

Option 5: This option is not correct. You should be the one to deal with Rania's difficult behavior. If you were to call Rania's supervisor, it would likely cause Rania to resent you, and you'd reduce your personal effectiveness in the negotiation.

In this topic, you've considered some examples for dealing with difficult people and learned about several strategies, including controlling your emotions, using assertive but gentle confrontation, seeking alternatives, and taking a break.

Question

How do you think you'll benefit from knowing how to apply these strategies for dealing with difficult people?

Options:

1. You'll be able to manipulate the negotiation to ensure your position prevails

2. You won't be thrown off balance when you must work with a difficult person

3. You'll be able to maximize your chances of achieving your negotiating goals

4. You'll be able to maintain your original position throughout the negotiating process

Answer

Option 1: This option is not correct. Your objective isn't to manipulate the negotiation, but rather to neutralize the effects of bad behavior. You don't want another person's behavior to make you ineffectual.

Option 2: This option is correct. Some negotiators use difficult behaviors to win their arguments. When you have techniques you can use to counter these behaviors, you'll be able to stay focused on your goals.

Option 3: This option is correct. When you don't let behaviors distract you or reduce your effectiveness, you'll be better able to achieve your goals.

Option 4: This option is not correct. Handling difficult people doesn't mean that you'll maintain your original position. It's unlikely that this will happen even when the other party is not being difficult.

CHAPTER 5 - AVOIDING PITFALLS IN NEGOTIATIONS

CHAPTER 5 - Avoiding Pitfalls in Negotiations
 SECTION 1 - Common Errors Negotiators Make
 SECTION 2 - Avoiding Negotiation Traps
 SECTION 3 - Diagnosing Barriers to Agreement in a Negotiation

SECTION 1 - COMMON ERRORS NEGOTIATORS MAKE

SECTION 1 - Common Errors Negotiators Make

Five common errors you should try to avoid in negotiation situations are failing to prepare adequately, succumbing to the urge to win completely, overconfidence, losing control of your emotions, and limiting your options. Any of these errors can cause you to mishandle the negotiation and not get what you want or need.

FIVE COMMON ERRORS

Five common errors

Negotiating can be difficult, and almost everyone, at some point, has slipped up. The following example illustrates a common error in negotiating. Jean-Francois hasn't had a salary increase in two years. His performance appraisals have consistently been good, so Jean-Francois thinks he deserves a raise. However, when he meets with his boss, Renee, to ask for more money, he is unprepared for her objections. He isn't really sure what to ask for, so he ends up settling for what Renee offers – which is nothing.

Jean-Francois made one of the five most common errors in negotiating:
- failing to prepare adequately – this was the error made by Jean-Francois when he went to negotiate for his salary,
- succumbing to an urge to win completely, or being too competitive,
- being overconfident and, therefore, underestimating the other party,

- losing control of your emotions, which can make it difficult to continue negotiations, and
- limiting your options before you negotiate.

FAILING TO PREPARE

Failing to prepare

The first common error is failing to prepare for the negotiation. It's astonishing that people go into negotiations without knowing what they want or what they're going to say, yet it happens all the time. As with almost everything else in life, preparation is key.

The very first thing you have to do when preparing to negotiate with another party is identify what it is you want. It's important to be specific, and it's helpful to write it down.

Next, think about what you're willing to give up – your concessions. Remember, when you negotiate, you must give up things you value to get other things you value more.

Last, identify your alternatives. An alternative is a powerful weapon. For instance, if a customer demands a lower price, and you can't give in on price, you could offer the alternative of a free full-service warranty. By making it clear this is the best you can offer, the other party will often accept the alternative. It's better than nothing.

After you've defined these elements for yourself, do the same for the other party.

Remember Jean-Francois? He was unsuccessful in getting a raise because he was unprepared. Well, Jean-Francois did some reading about negotiating techniques, and he's prepared now. Follow along as he meets with Renee.

Renee: Jean-Francois. What can I do for you?

Jean-Francois: I've been wondering whether the company will be giving out raises this year. I haven't had a raise in two years. My performance appraisals have been good, so I think I deserve an increase.

Renee: I agree with you. We've had a freeze on salary increases for about a year now. I hope this situation will ease soon. But I can't do anything yet.

Jean-Francois: Well, would you consider giving me vacation days instead? It would be a fair gesture for the company to offer vacation time in lieu of salary increases for their good performers.

Renee: That sounds fair, Jean-Francois. Let me check with Human Resources to be sure I can do this. But I'll push for it.

Preparation made all the difference in this negotiation. When Jean-Francois realized he couldn't get what he wanted, he asked for an alternative. And Renee was agreeable to it.

SUCCUMBING TO THE URGE TO WIN

Succumbing to the urge to win

A second common error that negotiators make is succumbing to the urge to win completely. Many people are naturally competitive, and in the heat of the moment, it's easy to get carried away by a desire to beat the other party and "win."

But when this happens, the negotiation can become a conflict that easily escalates. To reach a good outcome, you must control your competitive urge and seek a fair resolution for yourself and the other party.

Consider Ram and Jared. The two project managers are negotiating responsibilities for an upcoming project. Ram is determined to win the negotiation. He's prepared, and is ready to fight for some specific high-visibility tasks and for the two most experienced workers for his team. But as Ram begins to push for what he wants, Jared pushes back. The pushing escalates, and Ram is soon shouting his demands. Jared walks out of the negotiation and complains to their boss.

Errors and Remedies

Ram's determination to win turned the negotiation into a competition. He should have used persuasive techniques and left himself some room to maneuver by preparing to offer concessions or an alternative. He should also have suggested taking a break, so that both he and Jared could cool off.

Ram's determination to win ruined the negotiation with Jared. He was so adamant about getting what he wanted that he left himself no room to maneuver. To avoid this situation in your own negotiations, don't get too attached to a specific position. Be prepared to modify your position in light of the other party's demands and objections.

Also, use persuasive techniques. If Ram had considered Jared's views, wants, and needs beforehand, he could've decided what concessions to offer and what alternatives were acceptable. He would've known what was fair and been careful not to go too far. And he would have communicated his offer in a way that appealed to Jared's interests too.

Another useful technique for controlling an urge to win is to set periodic break points. Break points help you to pace yourself, and breaks give you opportunities to cool off when negotiations heat up.

BEING OVERCONFIDENT

Being overconfident
Another common negotiating error is being overconfident. Confidence is a good thing – it gives you courage to tackle difficult and uncertain ventures. Overconfidence, however, leads you to underestimate the other party, make incorrect assumptions, and jump to the wrong conclusions.

Just ask Farley. As vice president of sales at an insurance company, Farley is meeting with Katherine, who represents a large auto manufacturer. Farley wants to sell Katherine a new health insurance contract for her workers.

Farley's company is reputed to be one of the best insurers in the country. And Farley has gotten used to people calling him to ask if they can do business.

He assumes this will be another easy negotiation, considering his company's reputation and his knowledge that Katherine is new to her job. Moreover, he doesn't pay attention to what the competition has to offer, because he's used to getting clients easily.

Imagine Farley's surprise when Katherine demands lower prices, longer benefit terms, and lower dental co-pays. She's done her homework, and she knows what she can get from other insurers. Katherine is prepared to buy from a different company if she doesn't get what she wants from Farley. Ultimately, this is what she does – Farley fails to present a convincing case because he's so sure that Katherine will want to go with his highly respected company.

Question

What do you think happened here? What did Farley do wrong?

Options:

1. He made assumptions about Katherine's abilities and concluded that he had more power in the negotiation

2. He was forced to negotiate on terms he didn't understand

3. He allowed Katherine to speak for too long before countering her arguments

Answer

Farley's overconfidence caused him to underestimate Katherine, and to make incorrect assumptions about what she wanted. As a result, Farley was unprepared to meet her demands.

Option 1: This is the correct option. Farley's overconfidence led him to make an incorrect assumption about Katherine's needs – that she'd just buy whatever he offered. He concluded he had the upper hand and failed to prepare and to really listen to Katherine.

Option 2: This option is incorrect. There's no evidence Farley didn't understand the terms. The main problem here was overconfidence. Farley didn't really listen to

Katherine and failed to prepare properly for the negotiation.

Option 3: This option is incorrect. Each side should be given enough time to speak. The real problem is that Farley was so overconfident that he assumed he had the deal clinched.

To help overcome the error of being overconfident, be sure to check your assumptions and conclusions about the other party and yourself before you enter into negotiations.

Sometimes, overconfidence is a result of an organizational phenomenon called groupthink. Groupthink is a tendency among team or organization members to think the same way. People in a group often strive for consensus without critically testing or evaluating each other's ideas. They ignore alternatives and discount information that doesn't agree with what they think they know. As they become more isolated from reality, people make poor decisions because of their faulty beliefs and assumptions.

To avoid groupthink, it's important to think for yourself.

Challenge your own beliefs and assumptions, and don't accept common organizational knowledge without questioning it.

If you need help with this, you might ask a third party to help you evaluate your knowledge and assumptions. This person can play "devil's advocate" to point out the flaws in your assumptions.

After his meeting with Katherine, Farley asked his mentor to help him examine his thinking.

Farley found that he had bought into his coworkers' attitude of "we're the best," and he hadn't rigorously evaluated his company's services in comparison with the competition. Once Farley began to think for himself, he became better at negotiating.

LOSING CONTROL OF EMOTIONS

Losing control of emotions

A fourth common negotiating error is losing control of your emotions. Negotiations can produce very strong emotions of anger and fear. And in the heat of the moment, it can be hard to remain calm.

However, losing control of your emotions can cause you to forget the importance of logic and of your ultimate goal for the negotiation.

So what can you do when either you or the other party begins to lose control? There are some remedies. Don't escalate the situation with a potentially incendiary response. Wait and think before replying to the other party. Take a break so one or both of you can cool off. Try to understand your reaction. Then, if these remedies don't work, ask a third party to moderate the discussion.

Don't escalate – wait before replying

Rather than replying quickly to the other party during the discussion, pause before you speak. Think about your reply. By waiting, you can often prevent yourself from making an angry or sarcastic remark that would escalate into a conflict.

Take a break

Take a break and leave the negotiating table. Give yourself or the other person time to regain composure. During the break, think about what's happening and how you can change your strategies to achieve a more productive session.

Try to understand your reaction

Try to figure out why you're reacting the way you are. Maybe you're angry at a perceived lack of fairness. Perhaps you're fearful because you feel unprepared or overwhelmed. When you identify the causes of your emotion, you can often deal with it more effectively.

Ask a third party to moderate

If you and the other party in the negotiation are unable to negotiate rationally, you may want to ask a moderator to help you resolve your differences. A third party who isn't personally invested in the issues you're discussing will bring a cool and calm head to the negotiation.

Luis and Heidi share a job. Each of them works roughly 20 hours a week, but they often help each other out by working more or fewer hours, as needed. Luis is currently facing some problems at home. Follow along as he asks Heidi to take on some of his hours for the next month.

Luis: I have some issues to deal with on the home front. I can only work 10 hours a week for the next month. Is there any way you could pick up the slack for me?

Heidi: That means I could be stuck working 30 hours. I can't do that. I'm sorry. This is too much to ask.

Luis: But you're single. You don't have any other commitments.

Luis sounds angry.

Heidi: What? That's incredibly insulting. You're making assumptions about my life.

Heidi seems very angry.

Luis: Give me a break. You don't have a family, so you must have more time.

Luis is angry and resentful.

Heidi: If you are going to continue making assumptions about me, this discussion is over.

Heidi is furious, but sounds icy and calm.

Question

What could Luis have done to prevent Heidi from losing control of her emotions?

Options:

1. Luis could have paused and thought before making the remark about Heidi not having any commitments

2. Luis could have tried to understand his feelings about Heidi's marital status

3. Luis could have asked someone else to help moderate the negotiation

4. Luis could have asked someone besides Heidi to take his hours

5. Luis could have told Heidi to calm down

Answer

Option 1: This option is correct. Heidi responds somewhat emotionally to the request. And Luis escalates her emotion by verbalizing an assumption about her commitments.

Option 2: This option is correct. Luis may have been resentful about having family issues to deal with. He should have delved into those feelings before approaching Heidi.

Option 3: This option is correct. A third party could have intervened in the escalating argument and helped Luis and Heidi to come to an agreement.

Option 4: This option is incorrect. Luis and Heidi share the job, so Luis had to negotiate with her.

Option 5: This option is incorrect. This approach could backfire and make Heidi even more angry. Understanding where she is coming from is more important at this point.

If Luis had noticed Heidi was somewhat angered by his request, he might have paused to think before making thoughtless replies that increased her anger.

He might have realized that he was resentful of her single status and put more effort into thinking about the situation from her perspective.

LIMITING YOUR OPTIONS

Limiting your options

A fifth common error that negotiators make is limiting their options. One cause of limiting your options is absolute thinking. If you're someone who thinks in absolutes – black or white, all or nothing, win or lose – you may limit your chances for negotiating success.

Maya owns a service station. Follow along as she negotiates the price of auto parts with Victor, a supplier.

Maya: Hello, Victor. I need brake pads. What can you do for me?

Victor: I have some brake pads coming into the shop next week. The cost to you will be $65.00.

Maya: Is that the best you can do?

Victor: Afraid so. We do have a money-back warranty that comes with each part.

Maya: But the price is just too high. I can't accept that price.

Maya is assuming that Victor only wants the highest price from her, so she doesn't bother negotiating.

Negotiation Essentials

But consider this – Victor may be willing to reduce the price if Maya buys today instead of next week, or if she guarantees she'll buy a certain number of products over the next six months or year.

By assuming that Victor only cares about price, Maya may miss an opportunity to negotiate based on other facets of the deal.

It's important to think "outside the box," and be flexible. Identify aspects of the product or service – variables – that you might be able to use to make a deal. For instance, if you're negotiating the terms of a new job, you could negotiate a higher salary by trading in vacation time, or vice versa.

Another way that people sometimes limit their options is to believe that the other side has all the power.

Power is often communicated subconsciously. Before the actual negotiation begins, people check each other out, observing attitudes, demeanor, and style of dress, for instance. Often, based on this evaluation, one person gives up power to the other.

When this happens, the person who ceded power may automatically limit what is asked for.

To counter this tendency, you need to be aware of these kinds of power struggles while they're happening. While it's human nature to measure yourself against others, you shouldn't give up your power under any circumstances.

Remember that, in a negotiation, the rules of who has power are different from a normal work situation. Even if you're meeting with someone higher up in the organization who has more authority than you do, you have a legitimate right to negotiate as an equal simply by virtue of being at the negotiating table.

Question Set

Even the best negotiators make errors. It's important for you to know about the most common errors, so you can avoid them.

Question 1 of 2

Andy is negotiating with a sales rep for a large distribution company. What should Andy have done to avoid the errors evident in this negotiation situation?

Options:

1. He should have been prepared to answer questions about the games

2. He should have closed the deal before Hashem could bring up the platform requirement

3. He should have controlled his competitive urge and sought a fair deal for Hashem too

4. Andy should have called in a third party to moderate

5. Andy shouldn't have made assumptions about his reputation and about Hashem

Answer

Option 1: This option is correct. Andy didn't prepare for the negotiation by anticipating what Hashem might ask for. Moreover, he wasn't clear on the requirements of his own product.

Option 2: This option is incorrect. Letting the other side ask for alternatives or concessions is part of the give and take of negotiations. Andy should have considered the other side and not focused so much on winning.

Option 3: This option is correct. Andy wanted to win, and this led him to make a decision that ended the negotiations. This overarching competitive urge and his lack of preparation made his success unlikely.

Option 4: This option is incorrect. A third party is commonly used when two parties are unable to negotiate rationally. Andy doesn't lose control of his emotions here but instead becomes focused on the need to win, losing sight of the needs of the other party.

Option 5: This option is correct. Andy exhibited the common error of overconfidence, which led him to make assumptions and to underestimate Hashem.

Question 2 of 2

Sara is negotiating with a multinational bank. What should Sara have done to avoid the errors evident in this negotiation situation?

Options:

1. She should have identified variables other than price on which to make a deal

2. She should have insisted on her initial price

3. She should have controlled her competitive urge and sought a fair resolution

Answer

Option 1: This is the correct option. When Sara determined that price was the negotiating point, she ignored other variables. She might have been able to use these variables as bargaining points, and maintained a higher price.

Option 2: This option is incorrect. Sticking with the initial price doesn't show much flexibility. Sara is limiting her options by sticking to the issue of price – she really needs to be more flexible.

Option 3: This option is incorrect. Sara doesn't display an overconfident behavior. The main issue here is that she limits her options by focusing on price and needs to consider other variables to forge the deal.

SECTION 2 - AVOIDING NEGOTIATION TRAPS

SECTION 2 - Avoiding Negotiation Traps

Win-win negotiations are ideal, but they're not always possible. You should have strategies available to you for dealing with negotiation traps, such as unreasonable demands, take it or leave it attitudes, inadequate authority, and last-minute changes.

BENEFITS OF AVOIDING NEGOTIATION TRAPS

Benefits of avoiding negotiation traps

Win-win negotiations are the ideal, but they're not always possible. Sometimes, the other party simply won't cooperate. Tough negotiators often seek win-lose outcomes, and they'll set traps to keep you from negotiating effectively.

When you know how to avoid negotiating traps, you'll realize some important benefits. You'll be able to achieve a successful outcome in the face of adversity, you'll be more confident going into any negotiation, and you'll be able to keep negotiations on track.

Question

Marty was negotiating with Frieda, a very competitive person. Frieda did her best to dominate the proceedings, raising her voice and gesturing furiously to make her points. She made unreasonable demands, and presented the ultimatum "take it or leave it" more than once. Just as the negotiation was concluding, Frieda threw in a request that could have derailed the entire negotiation. Fortunately, Marty was able to counter Frieda's tactics.

What benefits do you think Marty derived from knowing how to avoid Frieda's negotiation traps?

Options:

1. Negotiating with Frieda gave Marty confidence to handle almost anything

2. He wasn't thrown off stride when Frieda made unreasonable demands and threw in a last-minute change

3. He was able to reach a successful outcome

4. Marty was able to calm Frieda down and change her behavior 5. He earned Frieda's respect

Answer

Option 1: This option is correct. After Marty concluded his deal with Frieda, successfully avoiding her traps, he was confident he could handle other difficult negotiators he might encounter.

Option 2: This option is correct. Frieda did her best to throw Marty off his game. Knowing how to deal with her traps helped him keep the negotiation on track at points when it could easily have ended badly.

Option 3: This option is correct. Knowing how to avoid Frieda's negotiation traps enabled Marty to close the deal.

Option 4: This option is incorrect. Marty couldn't change Frieda's behavior, but he could control his own behavior and avoid the negotiation traps she set for him.

Option 5: This option is incorrect. Frieda was counting on winning the negotiation. Marty's skill at countering her tactics likely didn't endear him to her. And the goal of the negotiation isn't to earn someone else's respect. This may happen as a result of you showing skill at negotiating, but it's not a direct benefit.

Sorin Dumitrascu

This topic covers strategies for countering difficult tactics from the other party in a negotiating situation. These difficult tactics include making unreasonable demands, adopting a take it or leave it attitude, claiming you have inadequate authority, and making last minute changes.

COUNTERING UNREASONABLE DEMANDS

Countering unreasonable demands

Have you ever faced a negotiator who makes unreasonable demands right at the start? Consider this situation. Bryce is calling on Saranya, a new customer, to introduce his service and sign her to a contract. Saranya walks into the negotiation and sits down. She says in a loud voice, "Let's not waste each other's time. I require immediate service for all our vendors. If you can't give me this, we're done here." Shocked, Bryce begins offering concessions.

This is exactly what Saranya was hoping for by opening with an unreasonable demand. Saranya caught Bryce off guard. He immediately lowered his expectations for the negotiation and offered concessions.

At that point, Saranya knew she'd won. There are several things you should avoid when you encounter an unreasonable demand.

First of all, don't offer concessions. If you do this, the other side will consider it a win and continue being unreasonable. And second, don't escalate the situation by making your own demands.

Instead, recognize that you're dealing with someone for whom negotiation is a test of wills and don't let the bad behavior throw you.

There are several strategies that can help you deal with unreasonable demands. One such strategy is to understand what's happening and be cautious with information; don't disclose too much. Another strategy is to restate the demand in your own words, but in terms that are acceptable to you. And a third strategy is to tell the person that the demand is unacceptable and then be prepared to walk away.

Be cautious with information

Sometimes, a hard bargainer will open with an unreasonable demand to provoke you to reveal important details, such as your bottom-line price. Remember, in a negotiation, anything you say can and will be used against you.

Imagine Stuart is meeting with Georgina, a vendor, to negotiate a price for a favorite coffee used in his restaurant chain. At the start of the discussion, Georgina states firmly, "The rains in South America have caused a shortage. The price is $2.35 a pound." Stuart knows he won't pay over $2.20 a pound, but he doesn't want Georgina to know this, so he says nothing and thinks about his options.

Restate the demand

Stuart wants to continue the negotiation, so to leave room for maneuvering, he decides to offer less than his best offer, which is $2.20 a pound.

He regards Georgina calmly and restates her demand in his own words, in terms favorable to him. He says, "Your price is $2.35 a pound. I'm prepared to offer $2.15 a pound."

Prepare to walk away

Georgina repeats adamantly, "That won't do. I need $2.35 a pound."

At this point, Stuart needs to show Georgina that he's serious about not accepting her price. He states firmly, but politely, "That price is unacceptable. Is that your final offer?" Stuart makes it clear that he's fully prepared to walk away from the negotiation.

Finally, concerned with saving the deal, Georgina softens and says, "Well, what's the best you can do?"

Dealing with an unreasonable demand can take some courage. It's unpleasant to walk away from a negotiation, but if it's the only remaining option, don't be afraid to do it.

COUNTERING A TAKE IT OR LEAVE IT OFFER

Countering a take it or leave it offer

A second tactic that tough negotiators use is to adopt a take it or leave it attitude. Why would someone use this tactic? It's often an attempt to undercut your feeling of power and competence, and to make you lower your expectations of success.

Consider what happened to Steve. Steve was in a critical negotiation for his company. After days of discussions, Sheila, the other party, gave him a take it or leave it offer. Steve was taken aback – they'd seemed to be working toward a common point. Even though Sheila's offer wasn't good for his company, Steve took it. His company lost money on the deal.

Question

Steve jumped at Sheila's offer because he felt he had to. Sheila successfully undercut his feeling of power in the situation, and he responded by lowering his expectations. He later found out that she uses this tactic often because it's so effective for her.

Which strategies do you think Steve could have used to counter Sheila's offer?

Options:

1. Restate his position and the benefits it provides to Sheila's company
2. Let Sheila know her offer is unworkable and unacceptable as it stands
3. Take a break to discuss the offer with a partner or another stakeholder who could help him
4. Offer his best alternative
5. Tell Sheila that he recognizes her bluff
6. Respond with his own take-it-or-leave-it demand

Answer

Effective strategies in this situation include restating your position and the benefits it offers; letting the other party know the offer is unacceptable; taking a break; and offering your best alternative.

Option 1: This option is correct. By emphasizing the benefits, Steve would have reminded Sheila that he was offering something of value to her.

Option 2: This option is correct. Sheila's offer may have been a power play. Steve should have let her know that her offer is unacceptable. Then he could have stated that he's willing to continue working toward a mutually satisfactory conclusion.

Option 3: This option is correct. Taking a break would have given Steve a chance to consult with a teammate or other stakeholder in the negotiation. A break can also change the pace of the discussion and equalize the balance of power that was thrown off by the offer.

Option 4: This option is correct. Steve should have been prepared to offer his best alternative in response to

Sheila's offer. Then, if she turned it down, he would have been able to walk away.

Option 5: This option is incorrect. Sheila may not have been bluffing. If Steve made this assumption, and had actually used the word bluff in relation to Sheila's offer, he may have lost the deal.

Option 6: This option is incorrect. If Steve had responded this way, it could have led to a deadlock or impasse in the negotiations.

When faced with a take it or leave it attitude, there are some effective strategies you can use. You can, firmly but gently, let the other party know that the offer is unacceptable. To do this, you might compare what's being given and taken by each side to give a clearer picture of a fair deal. You can also restate your position and the benefits it offers the other party. This will get the other party refocused on the positive aspects of your position and keep negotiations moving forward.

You could also take a break and consult with the negotiating team or another interested party who can help you. This can also help change the pace, preventing a bad concession.

Finally, you may need to indicate that you're willing to walk away. If the other side's offer is worse than your predetermined walkaway point, and there's an unwillingness to budge, you need to take action. If you don't take action, the other side may think its position is acceptable.

When you indicate that you're willing to walk away, the other party may decide to be more flexible.

COUNTERING INADEQUATE AUTHORITY

Countering inadequate authority

A third negotiating pitfall is when the person you're negotiating with claims to have inadequate authority to give you what you're asking for.

This can waste a great deal of your time and cause mental and physical fatigue.

And this is exactly what happened to George. George was negotiating union wages and benefits with Aiesha, who was acting on behalf of a hotel chain. After three days of negotiations, George thought they were finally approaching agreement, when Aiesha said, "I don't have the authority to close this deal. I have to run it by my boss." Exhausted and fed up, George reacted angrily to this revelation, and the negotiations ended on a negative note.

Aiesha had an "invisible partner" – her boss – who retained the authority for final deal-making.

George might have been able to avoid being taken by surprise if he'd done some research ahead of time – a necessary step to avoid falling into this negotiation trap.

Question

To avoid negotiating with someone who has inadequate authority, what kind of research do you think you should do?

Options:

1. Find out about the negotiator's position in the organization
2. Find out about the organization's decision-making process
3. Find out whether the negotiator's boss is a micromanager
4. Find out whether the negotiator has negotiating experience

Answer

Option 1: This option is correct. Often, a person's position can reveal something about authority level.

Option 2: This option is correct. If the organization's decision-making process involves levels of approval, you won't be making a final decision at the initial negotiation.

Option 3: This option is incorrect. The boss may have approval privileges, even if the boss is a micromanager.

Option 4: This option is incorrect. Even an experienced negotiator may not be authorized to finalize a deal with you.

Before going into any negotiation, you want to find out everything you can about the person you'll be negotiating with. For instance, the person's job title may tell you how much authority the individual has. An organizational chart will show you relevant reporting relationships.

You'll also want to investigate how decisions are made in the other party's organization. Some organizations require that all decisions are reviewed by an executive board or by managers of affected departments.

This research will help you prepare for the negotiation, but once you're face to face with the other party, you should also ask questions like these:

- What is your authority level for making this deal?
- Once we've reached our agreement, what happens next?
- How long does it normally take to get approval?
- Is there anyone else you need to consult in order to come to an agreement on our issues?

If you find there's an invisible partner who has the real authority to make the deal, ask to meet the individual.

Don't try to negotiate when you meet with this person, but do try to work in a discussion of the negotiation parameters. For instance, you may ask the invisible partner whether the person you're negotiating with has the authority to close a deal. Or whether you can contact the partner in the future with questions you may have. You can also ask whether the partner will be joining any of the negotiating sessions.

The more authority issues you can work out in advance, the more smoothly your negotiation will go.

But sometimes, even when you prepare and think you are with the person who has authority to close the deal, the other party may claim lack of authority as a strategy to get a better deal, or to stall negotiations.

In such cases, you need to control your emotions. This can be difficult if you've spent a lot of time in negotiations, working out details.

You also need to make it clear that the negotiations have reached a conclusion and that any changes will cause further delays, and possibly the end of the deal.

George felt betrayed that Aiesha didn't tell him she didn't have the authority to close their deal, but he could have handled the situation better. Follow along to learn what George should have said to her.

George: I didn't know that you don't have the final authority to make this deal, Aiesha.

George is serious.

Aiesha: No. My boss does. I'll run this by him and let you know what happens.

Aiesha seems embarrassed.

George: Aiesha, please be sure that you explain to your boss that we negotiated the deal to its conclusion. If he changes something, I'll have to take the deal back to my people, and they'll probably want to change something too. Changes will definitely hold things up. We may have to go back to the negotiating table.

Aiesha: I don't want that to happen, George! I'm sure he'll question things, but I'll do my best to keep him from making changes. We don't want to delay these new wage and benefit guidelines any longer.

Aiesha seems serious.

COUNTERING LAST MINUTE CHANGES

Countering last minute changes

It's not uncommon for negotiations to reach the finalization stage, only to have the other party request a last-minute change. The person doing this counts on the fact that you're tired and want to go home. You may have a carpool waiting or a flight to catch, and you don't want to put the settled negotiation at risk. But should you concede?

Actually, you should resist the temptation to give in. There are some strategies for countering a last- minute change. First, keep track of agenda items and issues as you go along. Then, isolate the change and treat it differently from the regular agenda items. Next, consider the cost of the concession compared to the cost of another day of negotiations.

Keep track of agenda items and issues

Your agenda should contain an agreed-to list of issues to be discussed. During the discussion, check off issues as you dispatch them. This practice will help to ensure you cover everything you intend to, and it will help you determine whether a last-minute change is or isn't an agreed to negotiation item.

Isolate the last-minute change

Don't include the last-minute change with the other negotiated items. Isolate and deal with it separately. You might say, "Let's discuss this at a later time." or "I'll document this as a new item and we can take it up next week."

Then document the change and your discussion of it. Sign or initial the document and have the other party do the same. This way, if there's a question about this issue, you'll have a record.

Evaluate the cost of the concession

Even though you're anxious to conclude the negotiation, resist giving in. Think about what the concession would cost your company in the long run. Another day of your time, another night in a hotel, and a few expense account meals might be nothing compared to that cost.

You may need more time to evaluate the cost, but stop and consider that it may be too great. This will help keep you from giving in, especially when you're tired after long negotiations.

Eli and Raheem have spent three tense days negotiating a contract extension for Eli's company. They've had some major disagreements, but the end is in sight. Eli wants to conclude the negotiations and head home. Fifteen minutes before Eli is due to leave, Raheem throws in a last-minute change. Follow along to learn how Eli handles it.

Eli: It's been an eventful three days, Raheem. It's too bad I have to catch a plane. Next time I'm in town, dinner's on me, OK?

Raheem: Before you go, there's one more thing. I think you should give us a deal on the equipment upgrade you've agreed to.

Eli: We discussed the equipment upgrade yesterday. Price wasn't on the agenda.

Raheem: Right. But my boss is looking for a 10% discount on the price. I can't close the deal without it.

Eli: I'm not happy with this sudden change, Raheem, but I'll write it into the contract.

Question

Which strategy did Eli apply effectively in this negotiation with Raheem?

Options:
1. He kept track of the issues
2. He isolated the last-minute change
3. He considered the cost of the concession
4. He resisted making the change

Answer

Option 1: This is the correct option. Eli kept track of the issues, and he knew that the price cut was not on the agenda.

Option 2: This option is incorrect. Although Eli recognized that the discount was a last-minute change, he included it in the contract anyway.

Option 3: This option is incorrect. Eli didn't evaluate the cost of the concession. He stated that he wasn't happy with this change, but he didn't state why. He needs more time to examine the issue.

Option 4: This option is incorrect. Eli gave in to temptation and made the change, even though he expressed his unhappiness about it.

Now you've learned about some important strategies for countering negotiation traps, such as unreasonable demands, a take it or leave it attitude, inadequate authority, and last minute changes.

Question

Now, match the examples of difficult negotiation tactics to the strategies that help address them.

Options:

A. Just before you're set to close a deal, Jane asks for higher benefit levels

B. At the start of a negotiation, Marcy tells you she doesn't have the authority to close a deal

C. At the end of long negotiations, Cary says he needs approval from the boss to close the deal

D. Tyson names a price and says, "It's as far as we'll go," but the offer isn't fair for you

E. Michelle makes an outrageous demand at the start of the negotiation

Targets:

1. Check your agenda items, isolate the change from the other negotiated items, and consider the cost of conceding

2. Ask to meet the "invisible partner" to discuss negotiation parameters

3. Remain calm and tell the other party changes made to a finalized deal could hold things up even further

4. Gently let the party know the offer is unacceptable, restate your position and its benefits, or take a break

5. Be cautious with information; restate the demand in terms that are favorable to you

Answer

You should resist the temptation to give in to last minute changes. Keep track of agenda items and isolate changes – document them but don't include them in the deal. Consider the cost of conceding.

If you find out the other party has an invisible partner, ask to meet this person and discuss the parameters of the negotiation.

It's easy to lose your temper when, after a long negotiation, the other party doesn't have adequate authority to make the deal. You must remain calm. Make it clear that changes made to any terms could hold up the deal.

When dealing with a take-it-or-leave-it attitude, let the other party know the offer is unacceptable; restate your position and its benefits to get the party thinking from your point of view; or take a break to talk to someone about how to approach the offer.

When faced with an unreasonable demand, try to understand what's happening; be cautious with information. Restate the demand in your own words, but in a way that's acceptable to you. In some cases, you may need to walk away.

SECTION 3 - DIAGNOSING BARRIERS TO AGREEMENT IN A NEGOTIATION

SECTION 3 - Diagnosing Barriers to Agreement in a Negotiation

To diagnose barriers to agreement in a negotiation, you need to look at the design of the negotiation, the negotiating session itself, and the structure of the deal.

BARRIERS TO AGREEMENT

Barriers to agreement

Have you ever been involved in a negotiation that stalled or ended badly? Do you know why it happened? Perhaps there was a lack of trust between you and the other party. Or maybe there was poor communication between you. Perhaps you weren't meeting with the right people to make the deal.

Negotiations are very complicated, and there are many reasons why they fail. If you sense that your negotiations aren't going well, you need to figure out why by identifying the barriers to agreement and then working to overcome them. It helps to focus on three main areas when you need to diagnose problems with a negotiation – the negotiation design, the negotiating session itself, and the pending deal.

You should check whether the barriers to agreement result from a flawed negotiation design. For instance, you or the other party may have misjudged the scope of the negotiation, or you may have followed a poor sequence –

in other words, the order in which you dealt with the issues may be causing problems in reaching an agreement.

Misjudged scope

If you don't have the right people at the table, you won't be able to reach a satisfactory agreement. Likewise, the people who are there must accurately represent the organization's positions.

For example, you're negotiating a work schedule for creating a new software game. Representatives from the Programming and Audio Recording departments are present, but no one invited Graphic Arts. The schedule you agree to won't be satisfactory because not all affected departments have given their input.

Poor sequencing

Sequence is the order in which issues are discussed. Proper sequencing helps ensure the discussion proceeds smoothly. It can create a momentum that leads to agreement.

If you don't pay attention to the order in which you discuss items in a negotiation, you may need to go back to earlier items to revise them, interrupting the flow of the discussion. The session may become overly long and difficult to follow.

For example, before you negotiate the number of units and when they will be delivered to a customer, you should discuss the product specifications. If you decide on a number and date before you know whether you can meet those specifications, you may need to go back and change the number of units and delivery date.

A second area to explore when barriers to negotiation surface is the negotiating session. When you meet face to face with others to negotiate a deal, you may encounter interpersonal issues or negotiating styles that impede progress.

Question

Which do you think are barriers that might surface during a negotiation?

Options:

1. Lack of trust
2. Poor communication
3. Fear of making the first move
4. Tough strategies
5. Failure to learn about the other party's wants and needs
6. Inviting the wrong people to the table
7. Failure to prepare an agenda
8. Cross-cultural conflicts

Answer

Barriers that surface during the negotiation are relationship-based or strategic. For instance, lack of trust, poor communication, cross-cultural issues, and fear of making the first move are relationship-based barriers. Using tough strategies is a strategic barrier.

Option 1: This option is correct. Lack of trust is a common relationship-based barrier.

Option 2: This option is correct. Poor communication is a common interpersonal problem in negotiations.

Option 3: This option is correct. Both parties may have information to protect, and may therefore be afraid to make the first offer in the negotiation. This is a tactical barrier.

Option 4: This option is correct. If the other party wants to win by forcing you to lose, it's very hard to reach agreement.

Option 5: This option is correct. Failure to find out what the other party's interests are or what the person wants from you can impede your ability to come to an agreement.

Option 6: This option isn't correct. This is a scope problem, which is a barrier that results from faulty negotiation design. It's a barrier that arises from a faulty set up for the negotiation.

Option 7: This option isn't correct. Preparing an agenda is part of designing the negotiation. It wouldn't be something that's done during the negotiation to create a barrier.

Option 8: This option is correct. Cross-cultural conflicts can impede communication and trust and keep you from reaching an agreement.

Barriers that arise during a negotiation are either relationship-based or strategic. For instance, lack of trust, poor communication, and cross-cultural conflicts are relationship-based barriers. Consider Peyton, who's negotiating the terms of a contract to install telephone equipment. The negotiations aren't going well. During a break, Peyton realizes why – the other party is slow to answer his questions and isn't forthcoming with information. Peyton thinks, "How can I make a deal with these people? They don't seem to trust me."

Barriers related to poor communication may arise if, for example, you don't present your ideas clearly, or you aren't listening well to the other side.

And if you're dealing with someone from a different culture, you may be misreading body language and cues. You may need to be more sensitive to cultural differences.

Strategic barriers can also arise during a negotiation session. These include the use of tough tactics, an inability to make the first move, and a lack of knowledge about the other side's interests and needs.

For instance, Drew is working with Gene to divide up some project responsibilities between them. Both parties stick to their positions – they want some of the same responsibilities and people for their teams.

This barrier relates to how the parties are approaching bargaining – neither side wants to budge from its position.

A third area to investigate for barriers to agreement is the structure of the pending deal. This barrier arises when one or both parties aren't satisfied with the terms of the deal that's on the table.

For instance, Kita and Richard have negotiated a contract for supplier services to its conclusion, but Kita isn't satisfied. She realizes that the price structure she agreed to isn't adequate. Now, the deal is nearly complete, but Kita is reluctant to finalize it.

While the deal you formulate may represent the "best you can do," if it doesn't give sufficient value relative to the parties' needs, or it fails to accomplish one or both parties' objectives, there's a problem.

Question

You're negotiating by phone to provide software services to a company in Sweden. There's strong potential for a good deal but you can't seem to get there. You've structured a deal, but neither you nor the other party seem to want to close on it.

Which steps can help you diagnose barriers to agreement in this negotiation?

Options:

1. Assess whether the right people are present at the negotiation
2. Consider whether you and the other party are satisfied with the terms of the deal
3. Prepare to walk away now before you get too invested in the negotiations
4. Take a more forceful approach in the negotiations and get the deal you need
5. Determine whether you're articulating your points clearly and that you're listening attentively
6. Consider the tactics that you're using to negotiate

Answer

Option 1: This option is correct. One of the steps in diagnosing barriers is to examine the set up of the negotiation – whether the correct people are present, and whether issues are being presented in the right sequence.

Option 2: This option is correct. One of the steps in diagnosing barriers to agreement is to consider the deal. As the deal develops, be sure that you're satisfied with the terms of the deal as you negotiate them. You don't want to arrive at the conclusion of the negotiation, only to find you're dissatisfied.

Option 3: This option isn't correct. This isn't a step in diagnosing barriers because you aren't trying to determine what's wrong. You're assuming that the negotiations will end badly and walking away from them.

Option 4: This option isn't correct. Being more forceful may create an additional barrier. Diagnosing barriers involves looking at the deal, the negotiation set up, and how the parties are communicating during the deal. Before taking action, you need to figure out why the negotiations aren't progressing well.

Option 5: This option is correct. One of the three areas you must investigate is the negotiating session itself. A common interpersonal barrier that can affect a negotiating session is poor communication.

Option 6: This option is correct. Diagnosing why there are barriers to agreement can mean looking at how you are approaching the negotiation itself. Are your tactics too strong or aggressive? Maybe you need to back down.

REFERENCES

References
1. **Practical Negotiating: Tools, Tactics, & Techniques** - 2007, Tom Gosselin, John Wiley & Sons
2. **How to Negotiate Effectively** - 2003, David Oliver, Kogan Page
3. **Successful Negotiating: Letting the Other Person Have Your Way** - 1998, Ginny Pearson Barns, Career Press
4. **The Negotiation Fieldbook: Simple Strategies to Help You Negotiate Everything** - 2005, Lum, Grande, McGraw-Hill
5. **Mastering Business Negotiation: A Working Guide to Making Deals and Resolving Conflict** - 2006, Roy J. Lewicki and Alexander Hiam, Jossey-Bass
6. **Negotiating, Persuading and Influencing** - 1995, Adam Fowler, CIPD Enterprises

7. **I Win, You Win: The Essential Guide To Principled Negotiation** - 2007, Carl Lyons, A & C Black
8. **Persuasion IQ: The 10 Skills You Need to Get Exactly What You Want** - 2008, Kurt W. Mortensen, AMACOM
9. **How to Become a Better Negotiator, Second Edition** - 2008, Richard A. Lueke and James G. Patterson, AMACOM
10. **Harvard Business School Essentials: Negotiation** - 2003, Harvard Business School Publishing, Harvard Business Press
11. **Black Belt Negotiating: Become a Master Negotiator Using Powerful Lessons from the Martial Arts** - 2007, Lee, Michael Soon and Sensei Grant Tabuchi, AMACON

GLOSSARY

Glossary

A

assertive language - Language that clearly and confidently states what you think and how you feel, standing up for your needs while acknowledging and respecting the other person's point of view.

avoider - A person who avoids conflict at all costs. An avoider is often a people pleaser and will avoid being straightforward if it means upsetting you.

B

BATNA - See best alternative to a negotiated agreement.

best alternative to a negotiated agreement - The most acceptable option for a negotiating party pertaining to its interests if the negotiations fail. A term created by Roger Fisher and William Ury.

bully - A person who tries to win through intimidation.

C

competitive negotiator - A person who approaches a negotiation as a win-lose contest and is determined to win at all costs.

compromising - A negotiating style in which a negotiating party sacrifices some of its needs for the sake of gaining other needs.

D

difficult person - Someone who puts up barriers to negotiation. Three types of difficult person are the bully, the avoider, and the competitive negotiator. See bully. See avoider. See competitive negotiator.

distributive negotiation - A type of negotiation that involves dividing up a fixed quantity, where a gain to one side results in a loss to the other. While both sides may benefit from the deal, one side will benefit more than the other.

I

integrative negotiation - A type of negotiation that involves a collaborative approach, where both sides work together in the hopes of achieving the greatest benefit for both sides.

N

negotiation - A process in which multiple parties with separate needs and expectations on an issue work to find a mutually acceptable solution.

P

persuasion -The art of swaying another party to your way of thinking, your belief, or your position.

persuasive strategies - Strategies that include putting yourself in the other party's position, building trust, and establishing a dialog.

primacy effect - A communication principle that states humans tend to remember the first thing heard in a list.

proposal - The tentative content of a potential decision in a negotiation.

R

recency effect - A communication principle that states people tend to remember the last thing heard, especially with long lists and difficult, or unfamiliar, points.

Z

zone of possible agreement - A range in which both parties involved in a negotiation can accept a deal.

ZOPA - See zone of possible agreement.

www.ingramcontent.com/pod-product-compliance
Lightning Source LLC
Chambersburg PA
CBHW020901180526
45163CB00007B/2580